LADY GREGORY:
A LITERARY PORTRAIT

At the height of her powers. A photograph taken in 1911, outside Hugh
Lane's house in Chelsea, by her niece Ruth Shine.

Lady Gregory

A LITERARY PORTRAIT

BY

ELIZABETH COXHEAD

HARCOURT, BRACE & WORLD, INC.
NEW YORK

Library of Congress Catalog Card Number: 61-13965
Printed in Great Britain

Preface

'THE greatest living Irishwoman' — so she was called by one who had good claim to be considered the greatest living Irishman; and if he had been asked to list the heads of her greatness, Bernard Shaw would certainly have put first her talent as a dramatist, which, as he had noted, was curiously like Molière's. In addition, she was co-founder and director of the Abbey Theatre, friend and hostess to all the principal figures of the Irish Renascence, her country's leading collector of folklore, perfector of the first Anglo-Irish prose idiom fully adapted to literary use, and a staunch fighter for intellectual and artistic freedom. As he wrote his praise, she was fighting the battle of *The Playboy* in America, having successfully defied Dublin Castle over his own *Blanco Posnet* two years before.

But within ten years of her death, a friend who was almost contemporary could write: 'I perceive no one in Ireland cares in the very least about her. She is almost forgotten already.'

She has never been quite forgotten, either in Ireland or in England. Her name is held in honour by innumerable amateur dramatic societies, who find her a mistress of that most difficult, and for their requirements desirable, form, the one-act play. But the professional stage largely ignores her, literary criticism has consistently belittled her, literary history has undervalued her part in the great creative upsurge which made Dublin the most important artistic capital of the early twentieth century. To many well-read people she is a name they may place if you give them time enough, eventually dredging up the clue 'Abbey Theatre' or 'friend of Yeats'.

And to my enquiries, one who is herself descended from

v

high colonial administration observed delightfully, though as it turned out not quite accurately: 'Ah yes, you mean the Governor's wife.'

To me also, she was a name and a single short play in the anthologies, until I chanced to set a novel in the Ireland or 1909, and in the course of background reading came on Lady Gregory. And then it required some strength of will to persevere with my own imaginings instead of listening to hers. For here, it immediately seemed to me, was a dramatic voice of unique and captivating quality; a voice with echoes of Molière, yes, but with the essential differences of being a woman's, and of being Irish; a voice with a wide range, from farce through humour and pathos to rueful tragi-comedy, and capable too of that occasional graver note that is never quite tragedy, but rather a maternal sense of the infinite pity of things.

I looked for a biography, but there was none; and when it came to piecing together the pattern of her fine, fighting life, I had to do it for myself, chiefly from the autobiographical material she has left in the prefaces to her books and the notes to her plays. One fact soon emerged that was of much encouragement in an age when we all live longer and longer, and grow ever more rapidly outmoded. Lady Gregory wrote her first fully creative work, her first actable play, when she was fifty.

This book does not pretend to be the documented biography that must be written one day, when all the materials are available. That is work for a scholar, preferably an Irish scholar, who can set her into the whole complicated perspective of the Irish literary revival, too close to us to be properly appreciated yet. I am English by birth and upbringing, and by trade a novelist, and my attention is focused on result rather than on cause: that is, on her writings and principally on her plays, though I have tried to give the facts of her life which have bearing on her plays in so far as I have been able to find them out. My hope is to dispel some of the ignorance which robs her of the credit that should be hers.

I believe that her plays are a source of pleasure and enrichment which we ought not to be missing; that they form the natural complement to those of Synge, whom we rob of a dimension if we ignore her; and that they should be brought back into circulation. Back on to the library and the reprint shelves; back into the common consciousness, quoted and chuckled over as they were in the Dublin of the nineteen-hundreds. Tried out freshly in the new medium of television, for which many of them, by their intimacy and delicacy, might almost have been designed. But above all, back to the medium for which they were intended, the creative vitality of the professional stage.

E. C.

Contents

List of Illustrations

Acknowledgements

I HAVE been generously helped in finding the material for this book, though I alone am responsible for the use I have made of it. I know that several of my conclusions will be disputed by some of my informants, and I tender to them my apologies.

I am firstly indebted to members of Lady Gregory's family. To her daughter-in-law Mrs Guy Gough, her grandson Major Richard Gregory, M.B.E., her nieces Mrs Farrell and the late Mrs Heaven (Ruth Shine), her great-niece Mrs E. M. Persse, her great-nephews Mr Dudley Persse and Mr Desmond Shawe-Taylor.

Then, to Mr Ernest Blythe of the Abbey Theatre, Mr A. MacLochlainn of the National Library of Ireland, Professor D. H. Greene of New York University, Professor D. J. Gordon of Reading University, Professor J. Murphy of University College, Galway, Dr Thomas Wall and Mr Ciaran Bairead of the Irish Folklore Commission, Mr Donnchadh O Suillebhain of the Gaelic League.

To Mrs Bagot, the late Miss Maureen Delany, Mr Gerard Fay, the late J. M. Hone, Mrs Hone, Miss Vivien Layard, Dr Thomas MacGreevy, Mr Brinsley Macnamara, Mr Micheal MacLiammoir, the late Dr Lennox Robinson, Mr Michael Walshe, Mrs W. B. Yeats.

To Mr and Mrs O'Brien of Gort, Father O'Callaghan and Mr O'Dea of Loughrea, Mr John Diviney of Kiltartan, Mr Paudeen Coneely of Inishmaan, the Editors of the *Connacht Tribune* and the *Galway Observer*, and the many other men and women in Lady Gregory's home county who went out of their way to help me.

To Messrs. John Murray (Publishers), Ltd. and Messrs. Putnam & Co., Ltd., for permission to quote from Lady Gregory's works.

I owe the photographs of Roxborough and Coole to Mrs Persse and Bord Failte, the photograph of Lady Gregory at Lindsey House to the late Mrs Heaven, permission to reproduce the J. B. Yeats portrait and the drawing of Douglas Hyde to the National Gallery of Ireland, and permission to reproduce the Epstein bust to the Dublin Municipal Gallery of Modern Art.

E. C.

I

Roxborough

The Persses of Galway were a branch of the Percys of Northumberland, and family tradition says that the first of them came into Ireland in Cromwellian times. The first of whom there is written record is Dudley Persse, who was in Anglican orders and rose to be Dean of the diocese of Kilmacduagh, acquiring from (ironically enough) the two English kings with Roman Catholic sympathies, Charles II and James II, extensive grants of land around Kiltartan and Kilchreest. 'The special merits which recommended Dean Persse to the favour of the Stuarts and the Irish executive are not set forth in history,' acidly remarks Dr Jerome Fahy, the Roman Catholic historian of Kilmacduagh, who does not like the Persses, and would probably have been even harder on them but for his long friendship with Lady Gregory. The Dean's portrait hangs today in the Californian home of his descendant, the present Dudley Persse, wearing, so its owner cheerfully avers, the expression of a thorough scoundrel.

The Dean built himself a mansion on the largest and richest of his properties, five miles from the little market town of Loughrea, and changed the soft Irish name of the place, Cregroostha, to the harsh Border one of Roxborough. At his death, the parish plate of the diocese was found to have disappeared, and rumour went that he had walled it up somewhere in his house. At intervals through the centuries the Persses probed fruitlessly for this treasure-cave, and after the house was burned down in the Civil War, the family returned for a last look. They were told it was useless; so strongly had the legend persisted that half the countryside had been there before them. It would seem that there were quite other reasons for the plate's disappearance, and that Dean Dudley was a maligned man.

The clan spread and prospered. Younger sons became soldiers, sometimes distinguished ones, but at heart the Persses were always gentlemen farmers, with an aptitude for getting hold of the best grazing land and making it pay. Ambrose Leet's *Directory* of 1814 lists five branches of the family in occupation of country seats in Galway, in addition to the reigning Persse of Roxborough, Lady Gregory's grandfather Robert. There is talk of evictions and ruthlessness; probably they were no worse than the general run of Anglo-Irish landlords; at best it is always a sorry story. They consolidated their position by intermarriage with landed families like their own, the Clanmorrises, the Goughs of Lough Cutra, the Shawe-Taylors of Castle Taylor, the Eyres of Eyrescourt, the Wades of Fairfield, eventually the Gregorys of Coole.

<h2 style="text-align:center">2</h2>

The nineteenth-century Dudley Persse was twice married, and the father of sixteen children, three by his first wife and thirteen by his second. Isabella Augusta, born on the 15th of March, 1852, was his twelfth child and youngest girl, but four more brothers followed her. He went each time for a wife to the family of O'Grady, marrying first the Honourable Katherine O'Grady, and then her cousin Frances Barry, daughter of Colonel Richard Barry of Castle Cor.

It must, I think, be with the O'Gradys that literary and artistic ability came into the family, the Persses having shown no flicker of it before that date. Standish O'Grady, first Viscount Guillamore, was a distinguished lawyer who rose to be Attorney-General and had the melancholy distinction of prosecuting Robert Emmet; he also enjoyed fame as a wit. And as well as a literary great-niece in Lady Gregory, he had a literary nephew in Standish Hayes O'Grady, one of the first scholars to translate from the early Irish texts.

It was likewise on the maternal side that Lady Gregory had a French great-grandmother, Françoise Algoin, the only one of her ancestors in whom she shows the smallest interest. She liked to think that she inherited 'moments of lightheartedness' and a feeling for the French classical comedy through this dash of French blood.

No writer can ever have been less parent-ridden. She has little to say of them, and what she does say is mostly unsympathetic; her mother always appears in a negative role, disapproving or forbidding. Dudley Persse survives in family tradition as a gouty old gentleman with one foot on a stool, brandishing a stick within radius of which no child might come.

Frances Persse, met by her son-in-law of the far distant future at a gay house-party in 1836, when he was an undergraduate and she not much older, is described as 'a very pretty woman not long married, dressed in white of an evening with pearl decorations'. But a portrait of her in middle-age shows a stern-faced Mrs Proudie, and there is no doubt that she 'considered the souls of the people', as did her elder daughters. They were proselytisers among their Catholic servants and tenantry, and Elizabeth, the eldest girl, after she had married the Shawe-Taylor heir, opened at Castle Taylor a proselytising school, which is qualified in Dr Fahy's book by the adjective 'notorious'.

It is difficult for a non-Irish and non-Catholic reader to appreciate the depth of bitterness with which this accusation of proselytism is still made in Ireland; to have been an evictor is almost preferable. It has its roots, of course, in the famine years, when a starving peasantry 'turned' for a bowl of soup. There is no suggestion that the Persse ladies ever took so cruel an advantage, or that they failed in charity towards any of their dependants; but converts were favoured when it came to giving out jobs, and orphans were brought up in a faith which was not that of their parents. And to this day it is believed by some in Ireland that the youngest daughter of the house must have shared in the work.

We have her own word for it that she did not, and when George Moore repeated the story in the first edition of *Ave*, she threatened to sue for libel and compelled him to withdraw it. She taught in the Sunday School attached to the little Protestant church on the Roxborough estate, but makes it clear it was Protestant children she was teaching. And the friendship extended to her by Dr Fahy and other distinguished Catholics would never have been given to one who had been known as a proselytiser.

Moreover, in an important unpublished reminiscence of her youth which she called *An Emigrant's Notebook* (I shall return to its literary significance later), she gives a half-amused but wholly disapproving account of her mother's activities, and how they resulted in characters like 'Honest John', with his determination that 'his religious convictions should be turned to the best advantage. He came to the village as a kind of squatter, taking possession of a tumbledown cabin, and on the following Sunday appeared at church accompanied by his wife and children, and driving before him two small pigs which he turned loose in the churchyard during Divine Service. "We have no sty for them," he said, "and no one to leave them with, and sure it's better to bring them than to stop at home ourselves from hearing the Word of God." The Mistress, always ready for any work of evangelisation, became a firm believer in the purity of his motives, and soon he was appointed her special workman, looking after her walks and

Roxborough House, with the slopes of Slieve Echtge beyond.

shrubberies, and was provided with a better lodging for himself and family, including a domicile for the two pigs whose attendance at church ceased forthwith. . . . He always professed a zeal for proselytism, and on the occasion of a visit from an unconverted brother I remember his coming to the Mistress to beg for a piece of bacon "just to tempt Francey to eat meat on a Friday and break with the old religion". But even the Mistress did not swallow this, or Francey the bacon.'

The *Notebook* was written during her marriage, and therefore may be held to show Sir William Gregory's influence, and he was a supporter of Catholic Emancipation and disapproved strongly of proselytising. And in the final instance, I suppose an accusation against a little girl that she copied her elders can never be completely answered. But I am satisfied that even as a little girl she was a rebel against the family thought and traditions; not a flamboyant rebel, but a quiet, dogged, persistent one, as she was to be all her life against what she considered unjust authority. And it was made the easier because she came so far down in that enormous family. They can hardly have noticed what she was up to. Indeed, one has the impression that for long periods of her childhood they hardly noticed her at all.

3

It was a happy childhood, in spite of the 'strict Orangism of the drawing-room'. Roxborough was a grand place to be a child in. The Dean's Stuart mansion had by this time grown into a great rambling L-shaped house; 'not beautiful,' she says, but photographs suggest otherwise. White-walled, with high-pitched gables, red blinds in the windows, green-painted windowboxes full of flowers, it must have had something of the charm of a French *manoir*. It was rat-ridden, of course, but so were all Irish country-houses; our modern insistence on a

B

rodent-free cosiness would have seemed very finicking to the families of the Ascendancy. There had been an attempt to Gothicise, which fortunately ran out with the building of a gatehouse and two bogus towers — doubly unnecessary because there were three genuine ruined towers, relics of the De Burgos, dotted about the estate.

But if she did not notice the charm of the house, she certainly appreciated what she calls 'the wide beauty' of its setting, in a demesne of grassy limestone hillocks; bounded to the east by the level line of the Slieve Echtge moorlands, open and airy to the west, so that by climbing a little one could see the Burren hills queerly armoured in their white limestone pavements, and catch a glimpse of the distant Atlantic.

A brown trout-stream flowed through the three-mile length of the demesne, artificially widened to form a lake before the house. And when, as an old woman, she underwent an operation that brought her close to death, her dream under the anaesthetic took her back to that stream, and along every stretch of it, past the nests of coots and wildfowl, past the house, the farm buildings, the millwheel, past the otters' caves and the bed of soft mud 'of which we children used to make little vessels that never went through the baking without cracks', through the woods to the high road that bounded the estate on the southern side, and so to the last underground journey that would take it, like all the other rivers of the district, through a limestone tunnel into Galway Bay.

She loved the three-acre garden. Strawberries were planted close to the path, so that 'sauntering along in apparent abstraction and without any appearance of greediness pre-pense you might stretch out your hand and take your fill of fruit as you walked'. The walls were covered with pears, cherries and peaches, and 'beyond the walls one could see the low green hills and the brown heather, and the woods where we knew lay uncounted heads of quickly startled wild deer —

once even I have seen an eagle soar over my head as I lay in the soft untrodden moss'.

She loved the little church, 'not a bad one as Irish churches go,' which stood in the demesne about a mile from the house, and had large square pews for the few squires' families, benches for the handful of police, gamekeepers and village folks, 'most of them Dissenters, but in Ireland a Protestant is a Protestant, all sects join hands in face of the common foe. . . . Our parish clerk was a Wesleyan, and gave out the hymns with an unction that would have satisfied a Cornish congregation.' Through the low windows young eyes could glimpse an occasional pheasant running in the long grass, and a visitor who remonstrated with the sexton on the state of the churchyard was answered with an indignant: 'And what would the Master say if I wor to disturb the young pheasants?' At christenings a white china basin was used as a font, but these events would become progressively rarer as the Protestant population failed to hold its ground. Today, all trace of the church has gone.

But best of all she loved the life and stir of a great working estate, a complete community within itself, comprising a dozen different trades. For the Persses lived off their land. Other sources of family income came and rather spectacularly went, but the six thousand acres of first-rate grazing, the vast herds of cattle and sheep (the shearing took a week), were what kept them in comfort, if never in real financial affluence.

The estate had its own smithy, sawmill, and carpenters' workshops; its coach-houses, cow-houses, dairy, laundry, piggery, kennels. And there was no genteel pretence of keeping these important departments in the background. They were built close to the house, so that everything went on under the Master's eye — and those of his children. The yard at Roxborough was a microcosm of the outside world. There could not be a better place for the future writer of dramatic fiction to absorb her knowledge of human nature, subconsciously and intuitively, as we only do in childhood. One thinks of George Eliot, driving round with her land-agent father, and gaining her incomparable insight into the Midland farming mind. No subsequent, deliberately acquired information can ever parallel the vitality of this, and the lack of it, in authors brought up in town flat or suburban villa, is surely one of the most serious deprivations of the present writing age.

The child's direct link with the world outside the drawing-room, and indeed the most important person in her life, was Mary Sheridan, for forty years nurse in the family. She was an Irish-speaker, and a walking library of fairytales and folk-lore, and she was moreover a link with the past, for she could remember the cheering at the news that the French had landed at Killala in 1798. 'After that she had lived as nursemaid in the family of Hamilton Rowan; she would tell us sometimes of his escape from prison, in which he was aided by his heroic wife, and of the boatmen from whom he tried to hide his face till one of them said: "We know you very well, Mr Rowan, and the reward that's on your head, and there is no fear that we will betray you." ' Here plainly is one thread leading to *The Rising of the Moon*.

'She was a good Catholic,' her nurseling writes of Mary Sheridan, 'though we heretic children often said our prayers at her knee.' Not the least valuable of the lessons learnt from her was what one might call the folklore side of Catholicism, so that the future Lady Gregory, though all her life she would remain the staunchest of Protestants, could yet enter imagina-tively into the minds of Catholic peasant characters, and transpose the gentleness of Irish saintly legend into religious plays acceptable to Catholic and Protestant alike.

At the time of the Fenian rising, Mary Sheridan had a discreetly veiled sympathy with the rebels, and the child found herself torn between the worlds of above-stairs and below. The boys were taught to shoot — might there not be rebels hiding in the woods or haylofts? — and she demanded permission to learn with them, though 'my gun was never loaded with anything more weighty than a copper cap'. Yet her imagination was caught by the dream of national freedom, and when she had earned sixpence by saying her Bible lesson without a mistake, she would take it to the old dark stationer's shop in Loughrea (it is still there) and standing on tiptoe at the counter receive in exchange a green-bound Fenian pamphlet or book of doggerel ballads, the first crude awakening of the new national literature. 'Perhaps but through the natural breaking of a younger child of the house from the conservatism of her elders,' is her modest explanation of her curious taste; but in that case, why should she alone of the sixteen children have possessed it? There were the makings of a rebel in her brother Frank, but with him the move was into rebelliousness of conduct — he eventually committed the arch-crime of marrying a Catholic — rather than into independence of thought.

This brother, and her sister Arabella, the two nearest to her in age, were the dearest to her of the family. (Another sister was called Adelaide, and another brother Algernon; Mrs Persse seems to have had a liking for grandiose Christian names beginning with A.) She also writes affectionately of her step-brother Dudley, 'the oldest of my father's sons,' who must have been more like an uncle. He was a military bachelor, who had fought at the Alma, and according to nursery legend killed seven Russians there. When Augusta married, he gave her as wedding-present the light phaeton which was to make folklore-collecting history; and in later years he would pay long visits to Coole, sitting on a bench in the garden, giving no heed to the literary brouhaha around him, but dreaming, taciturn, of his battles long ago.

4

Roxborough was a totally unbookish house. There was no library, and no encouragement for the interchanging of ideas. 'As a child our drawing-room evenings were not for conversation,' she says in the preface to *The Kiltartan Poetry Book*, 'the elders of the family keeping what little talk there was between piano-playing and newspapers to themselves; and I the youngest girl, at the fireless side of the round table, was glad enough to be seen and not heard, to win what glimpse of literature I could from the few books that lay there.' They were chiefly ornamental books; the nearest thing to a 'glimpse of literature' was Moore's *Lalla Rookh*; though elsewhere she speaks of a few old epics and histories, and it was perhaps at Roxborough that she got her love of Malory. Generally, however, she was starved of books, and reduced to borrowing from the village schoolmaster, whose stock cannot have been extensive either.

None of the children seem to have been sent away to school. The girls had an English governess, and the boys a tutor, and if the girls were unco' guid under Mrs Persse's evangelising eye, the boys compensated by a wildness and indiscipline which are still legendary in the county. They grew into Charles Lever Irishmen, magnificent riders, dead shots, passionate supporters of the local foxhounds, the famous Galway Blazers, founded by a cousin. (One of the pack's early festivities was so enthusiastic that the hotel where it was being held was burned down, hence the nickname.)

Half-hearted attempts were made to provide some of them with a university education, but naturally, with no previous training in intellectual discipline, they failed to profit by it. Frank spent his time at Trinity College making a collection of Dublin street-ballads, which Yeats in later years would try to get from him in vain.

Of the governess, or more probably, string of governesses,

nothing seems to be remembered. They may have laid the
foundations of the good French and German and competent
Italian Lady Gregory had, or she may have acquired these
entirely during the travels of her married life. One result of
Mary Sheridan's stories, and of the mysterious language she
daily heard spoken around her, was an eager wish to learn Irish.
'I thought to get leave to take lessons from an old scripture-
reader who spent a part of his time in the parish of Killinane,
teaching such scholars as he could find to read their own
language in the hope that they might turn to the only book
then being printed in Irish, the Bible. But my asking, timid
with the fear of mockery, was unheeded.' Irish was not a lady's
language; it was uncouth, something only servants spoke.

A second opportunity came and went, a visit from
Standish Hayes O'Grady, the scholar kinsman. But he
appeared to be taking a fancy to one of the elder daughters,
and Mrs Persse, who had a great objection to the marriage of
cousins, sent him packing.

But if intellectual companionship was lacking at Roxborough, there was plenty of the robuster kind, and it is plain
that she was happier with the naughty younger brothers than
with the prim elder sisters. The merriest recollections in the
Notebook are of holidays at Chevy Chase, a shooting lodge
the family had built high up on Slieve Echtge, scantily
furnished with 'stags' heads and horns and prints after
Landseer, and with three baskets of heather, hanging from
the ceiling and replenished once a year'. Here she would go
as deplorably amateur housekeeper to her brothers on their
shooting-parties, taking as much cooked food with her as
possible from the Roxborough kitchens; attempts to roast a
joint on the spit herself nearly resulted in setting the thatched
roof on fire, so that water had to be poured down the blazing
chimney, and the joint was burnt on one side and drowned on
the other. Yeats in *Dramatis Personae* speaks of a Trinity friend

of Frank's who was attracted by her, and whom once again Mrs Persse sent packing; she certainly had a firm way with undesirable suitors. But shy though Augusta might be in company, she learnt from her brothers how to relish and how to handle masculine society, and to the end of her life she always had a certain weakness for a rake.

5

The elder daughters had their seasons at the viceregal court in Dublin, and duly made their suitable marriages. Adelaide, the beauty, for whom great things were hoped, insisted on engaging herself to a penniless clergyman named Lane. ('I don't like those sort of names, Lane and Street and Field,' old Mary Sheridan was heard to grumble, 'they are apt to be given to foundlings.') For once in a way Mrs Persse was unable to send a suitor packing; the marriage was made, and was as unhappy as everyone had foretold; but it did result in the birth of that strange genius *manqué*, Hugh Lane.

If Arabella and Augusta were also given viceregal seasons, I have found no mention of it. Indeed, Lady Gregory's statement that till the founding of the Abbey she scarcely knew Dublin would bear out that they were not. Perhaps funds were low, or perhaps the youngest girls were considered too plain and insignificant to be worth making an effort for. And yet Augusta cannot have been plain. As a girl she was slender, and the fine eyes, of a curiously bright brown, the noble brow and well-carried head that gave her such distinction as an old woman, must in youth have given her the charm of an intelligent wood-nymph. But she was small, and the taste of the time inclined to large queenly women, such as Adelaide was.

At all events, she passed from girlhood to young-ladyhood, and presently into a state of being more or less on the shelf, all without going much outside the confines of the demesne;

one thinks of Anne Elliot, who had been 'too little from home, too little seen'. And like Anne but with a good deal more vitality and determination, she made her life a useful one. She became what amounted to a voluntary social worker on the estate. Besides her Sunday-School teaching, she took part in a scheme to get village libraries going, and Yeats speaks of her establishing a shop and selling in it herself, in order to compel the local shopkeepers to bring down their prices. She visited the cottages, and found much to remedy there. One of her early visits was to a girl dying of tuberculosis;

'She was lying in bed in a little room, quite dark. The window, being without frame or glass, had been boarded up. I was happy enough to be able to render her a true service, for I at once went to the steward about it, and so worked on his feelings that he gave me leave to try what I could do with the old carpenter, dry and hard as one of his own shavings. . . . It was not easy to get him to undertake any job not likely to bring in money, but this time he was ready and willing to help me. It was work for one who was poor and sick and of his own class, and a few days later I had the happiness of finding the dying girl no longer lying in the dark, but with the sunshine resting on her bed, and the trees and the sky to look at. . . . It was always a pleasure to me after that, if I found a windowless room in one of the houses, to have the want remedied. That was a sure way of doing good — it must always be good to let in light.'

Letters were brought to her to be read, and to be answered. Most families had emigrant relatives in America, who faithfully sent back money, and often outward passages for younger brothers and sisters. 'Each girl who went out usually sent home a highly flattering daguerrotype, with gold chain and rings and ornaments unmistakeably painted in to order, and these portraits formed the pride of their old dwellings.'

And so, instead of being anglicised by an alien education, as most young people of the Irish upper classes were, she continued the only sort of education that matters to a writer, learning to know and feel intensely her own small corner of the world. There is plenty of time later for travelling, and collecting local colour and background material, most of which is in any case futile — the sort of thing a writer falls back on when his creative days are over.

6

When she was twenty-seven, and hopes of finding a *parti* for her had probably been abandoned, her eldest full brother, Richard, fell ill, perhaps of tuberculosis. At all events the illness was to prove fatal. Doctors recommended the south of France, and Mrs Persse took him to Nice, taking Augusta also to share in the nursing.

At Nice they met their neighbour Sir William Gregory of Coole, recently retired from the governorship of Ceylon. He was an elderly but still extremely eligible widower, for whom the single women in Galway county society had been sighing in vain. Naturally he showed attention to his old friend in her sad plight. But what must have surprised everyone was his taking notice of Augusta, the shy bookish mouse. No doubt Mrs Persse did what she could to further the affair; one is told that when Sir William moved on to Rome, he found the Persses there before him. But it was Augusta's own eager longings after the world of literature and culture, of which he was a part and of which she knew so little, that touched the great man.

When they returned to Galway, it still seemed that a merely fatherly interest was being taken in her by one who was easily old enough to be her father. But he found that she was hungry for books; Coole had a fine library, and he gave her the run of it. And presently, having occasion to make a new will, he left her her choice of any six books from its shelves.

The next time he made a will, the whole library was hers, for by then she was his wife.

II

Marriage

===◇◇◇◇◇◇◇◇◇===

I

When a woman of twenty-eight marries a man of sixty-three, there must always be speculation as to whether she has done it 'for an establishment'; but I hope it will be conceded that a man of exceptional qualities might still be loved for himself. Fortunately we know what sort of man Sir William Gregory was. He has left, in his *Autobiography*, a self-portrait as vivid as it is honest, and one which in these days of Trollopian fervour some publisher should have the wit to re-issue. Trollope was his contemporary at Harrow, and it is not fanciful to see in him the model for one of the brilliant spoiled-darling heroes, Lord Lufton perhaps, or Frank Gresham.

His story has all the accoutrements of a Trollope 'political': the friendships of older statesmen for the young hero, the tug between personal and political loyalties, the great hostesses pulling wires, the costly elections, the lure of racing and gambling, the names unwisely set to bills for friends, even a duel to crown all. The central figure of these adventures eminently deserves the epithet manly, that favourite Trollopian adjective of praise. His faults and follies are the open and generous ones, and when he has to face their consequences, he does not whine.

He disclaims any interest in the family history, but proceeds to give a lively summary, which, with the subsequent researches of his kinsman Dr Vere Gregory, has made the essential information about the Gregorys easy of access. They were an ancient Warwickshire landed family, and as in the case of the Persses, a younger son came into Ireland with Cromwell. His two sons distinguished themselves by their courage at the siege of Londonderry, but it was the grandson of one of these, Robert Gregory, who really laid the foundation of the Irish branch's fortunes. His maternal uncles traded to India from Galway City, and as a schoolboy he stowed away on one of their ships, and was not discovered till it was too late to send him home. Arrived at Calcutta, he was given a writership in the East India Company, and by sheer ability rose to be director and finally chairman. This was the profitable era of Clive and Hastings, and he was able to retire to Galway as a man of great wealth, to buy large tracts of land and build Coole Park.

The wild schoolboy turned out, as so often happens, a stern parent to his own three sons. The eldest followed in his footsteps in India, but was disinherited for cock-fighting, an addiction most unluckily betrayed to his father by a Zoffany print in a Strand shop-window, showing a cock-match in progress at Lucknow and young Mr Gregory prominent in the foreground. The second son loved a penniless orphan and did not dare marry her during his father's lifetime; he hid her, disguised as a boy, in the steward's house at Coole, and there she passed into Coole folklore as 'Jack the Sailor', and was 'near killed with the lonesome', Lady Gregory was told long afterwards. The sad lover seems to have been the most cultivated of the Gregorys, and built up the splendid library at Coole.

That left the third son, William, to do the family credit, by marrying an earl's daughter and becoming Under-Secretary of State for Ireland — in fact, for practical purposes the ruler of the country, since he held office for nineteen years, under many changes of Lord Lieutenant and Chief Secretary, and all were guided by his probity and experience.

The Under-Secretary's eldest son, Robert, was a retiring and diffident man, the only Gregory content to live quietly at Coole, where he died of famine fever, caught through ministering to his tenants in the terrible years. The future Sir William was the only child of this Robert, but seems always to have been more the child of his energetic grandfather than of his shadowy father. He was born on July 13th, 1817, in the Under-Secretary's Lodge in Phoenix Park, a delightful house which is now the Papal Nunciature, and one of his early friends was Lord Wellesley, a Lord Lieutenant who inspired awe in everyone else but was grateful to learn from William Gregory where to catch the best roaches in the viceregal lake.

The boy was sent to an English preparatory school and then to Harrow, and spent all but the long summer holidays with his Warwickshire relations, so that he grew up English in manner, accent and outlook, like so many of his class. He was a brilliant classical scholar, described by his Harrow tutor as the cleverest boy he had ever handled, but a weakness in his character — or perhaps in his only-child position — presently revealed itself. Nothing succeeded with him like success, and he was usually successful; but equally, nothing failed like failure, for a setback would discourage him entirely. At Harrow he sulked for a term because another boy outshone him. At Oxford, more seriously, he sulked altogether, got into a fast set, and developed his fatal love of the turf. Desperate last-minute cramming brought on a breakdown, and he never took a degree, but instead won £5000 on 'Coronation' in the Derby of 1841 — quite an achievement for an undergraduate.

Politics were the next step: he was elected in 1842 as Conservative member for Dublin City, at a cost of £9000 in 'gratification' to the voters; one supporter asked him for a Government post afterwards, on the ground of having voted for him under thirteen different names. The great Daniel O'Connell, supporting his opponent, was captivated like everyone else by the young man's charm, and after he had taken his seat as a Peel back-bencher, used constantly to beckon him across the House for a chat, saying: 'If you could only see yourself in a glass, my dear boy, how much better you look than over the way, you would never go back to those fellows.'

The attraction was mutual. 'O'Connell always exercised a strong fascination over me,' he recalls. 'His humour and his passion carried me away. I always felt that he had led his countrymen out of the house of bondage and made them free men; and if his language was at times violent, abusive, and odious, God knows he was only giving back what he got.'

These sentiments had, of course, to be concealed from Sir Robert Peel, who treated young Gregory as one of the family, was delighted with his early speeches, and four years later offered him the Irish Lordship of the Treasury. But his father advised him to decline it, considering him too immature. It was a great mistake; Peel lost interest in him; once again he was discouraged, and Newmarket regained its hold.

His father's death in 1847 sent him back to famine-stricken Galway, where appalling sights met his eyes; but still he 'preferred the prospect of wiping off all liabilities by some stroke of good fortune on the turf to steady economy and supervision'. Everything went wrong: he lost his seat at the next year's general election; he signed bills for a friend who decamped to America; a racing quarrel with a Captain Vaughan resulted in what was probably the last duel fought on English soil.

The antagonists met at Osterley Park, the Villiers younger sons being friends of Gregory's. 'We were placed at twelve paces and ordered to fire at the word of command. My opponent's bullet sung close to my ear; I raised my pistol, took deliberate aim, by way of giving him a comfortable moment, and then fired into the air. They said they did not require a second shot, and so we went home on our way rejoicing. . . . The burning of powder clears the air, and so it was in this case. After the pistols were fired I had not a particle of enmity left, though my opinion of the transaction remained the same.'

(The late Lord Longford, Dublin's theatre-owning peer, was told by his grandfather, the Earl of Jersey, how as a small boy he remembered seeing from his nursery window at Osterley gentlemen in black going to fight this duel — a curious and romantic link between the generations.)

To get straight with his creditors, he was now obliged to sell all the outlying parts of the Galway estate. What had once brought in a rental of £7000 a year would henceforward be mainly a pleasure estate, and it would be necessary for the reigning Gregory to earn his living in the world beyond. And the results of the sale opened his eyes to the wretched position of the Irish tenant farmers. As Gregory tenants they had prospered; the new landlord doubled their rents, and ruined them.

When he re-entered Parliament in 1857 as member for Galway City — this time elected on his merits and wide popularity — he found himself far more nearly Liberal in his views. It now seemed to him 'one of the greatest evils of Irish society that the great mass of the agricultural population should be divorced from all ownership in the soil'. He was never a Home Ruler, believing that the prosperity of the two countries was too closely bound up, but he began a vigorous campaign for tenant security and for land purchase (which his nephew-by-marriage, John Shawe-Taylor, would ultimately carry to fruition). He offered his own remaining tenants the right to purchase, but he was so good a landlord that they all preferred to remain as they were.

He was also a supporter of Catholic Emancipation, because 'I had no objection to a State Church, both in England and in Ireland, but I had the strongest objection to a State Church of a minority'. Moreover, Roman Catholicism was, he thought, the only religion that could control 'the unruly wills and lawlessness of the Irish lower classes'. His aim was a contented peasantry and yeomanry, not mob-rule, of which he had a horror, reinforced by a visit to an America rife with the excitements made familiar to us by Western films.

He had always taken an interest in art, and had a natural flair for recognising Old Masters. Trusteeship of the National Gallery, and chairmanship of the committee appointed to reform the British Museum, brought him the friendship of Henry Layard, the excavator of Nineveh, who was now passing from a political to a diplomatic career, and this was to prove the closest intimacy of his life.

But he knew now that the great political positions would elude him, and after the passing of the Reform Bill he began to look around for a change of occupation. A colonial governorship would, he felt, suit, and he fixed on Ceylon, perhaps because Layard's cousin Charles was already high in the legislature there. He spoke to Lady Waldegrave, a powerful political hostess who was his friend, 'and she at once, and successfully, betook herself to obtain the promise of it from Lord Granville'; it was as simple as that. He married a wealthy young widow, to whom, he says, 'I had been deeply attached for many years of trouble to her,' and early in 1872 they sailed for Ceylon.

As Governor he was in every way a success. Benevolent despotism suited him far better than parliamentary manoeuvering; as he wrote to Layard: 'It is such a comfort when you find things going wrong to be able to set them right with the strong hand.' He started the building of the great breakwater which was to turn Colombo into a major port, he repaired

Coole: the entrance front.

Coole: the west front. The left-hand bay was the drawing-room, the right-hand the dining-room, with the library between them. The guest-room converted as a writing-room for Yeats was above the library; its window is concealed by the right-hand bay.

the irrigation system, widened the roads, reduced the drinking-shops, established small rural dispensaries on the Irish system of medical relief. Everything went well — till the adored young wife went out imprudently in the sun, and died. Once again he was discouraged; the loneliness became too much for him. But the visit of the Prince of Wales was a diversion, as well as a rather trying responsibility, and after it he was created K.C.M.G.

At the end of five years he resigned his governorship, another bad mistake, as he was soon acknowledging to Layard; for he was still at the height of his powers, the work had suited him ideally, and he had put himself out of public life. As always, the friendship of Layard, now British Ambassador at Constantinople, and his wife Enid was a consolation. He was making a leisurely journey towards them, via the south of France and Italy, when he encountered the Persses, with the results that we have seen.

'A man of great natural abilities, real political talent, and marked personal charm. But for a certain inherent instability he might easily have attained to the most eminent political positions.' The stately summing-up in the *Dictionary of National Biography* is fair enough. But it is impossible to come to his book's end without being slightly in love with Sir William Gregory; and I for one am convinced that Augusta Persse, despite the difference in their ages, loved him deeply, because he was far and away the most vital and intelligent person who had come into her world.

2

'Yesterday, the anniversary of my marriage, half a century ago!' she writes in her journal for 1930. 'So fresh still in my memory, the threshold of twelve such happy years! I looked younger than my age, so very slight — "She is a mere child," Lady Halliburton delighted William by exclaiming. And

c

Lady Somers begged him to take a supply of some forerunner of Bovril, I forget what, to sustain me on the journey to Rome and Constantinople. . . .'

They were married on March 4th, 1880, at St Matthias, Dublin, and the bride wore a simple travelling dress of grey. It was in every way more suitable, considering the bridegroom's age, and the fact that she was still in mourning for her brother. But she regretted it afterwards. 'The conventional dress of a widow has been mine, but never the dress of a bride.'

His letter to Layard from Paris, a few days later, gives the picture of a happy, teasing relationship between them. 'I am hardly recovered as yet from the surprise which my marriage has caused me. My wife, who was quite a student, is now plunged among *chiffons* and *modistes*, and I am bound to admit that she bears the infliction with a resignation which is rather alarming and ominous, excusing her new-fangled interest in dress on the grounds of pleasing me.' Evidently Cinderella got her finery after all.

Her welcome from the Layards was as warm as his had always been, and for Enid Layard, her ideal of a hostess and great lady, she felt a hero-worship which developed into the closest intimacy she ever had with another woman. To Lady Layard's literary antecedents I will return.

They were only just in time to see Sir Henry in his ambassadorial glory, for his diplomatic career was coming to an abrupt end. A confidential despatch, in which he gave his frank opinion of the Sultan's incompetence and personal cowardice, was published by the Foreign Office, whether through carelessness or treachery is not known. Queen Victoria, a strong supporter of monarchical trade-unionism, was scarcely less furious than the Sultan, and Sir Henry was not only recalled, but lost his hope of a peerage, in which matter, one is told, Sir William had been acting as intermediary. However, the Layards were childless and comfortably off, and had some years previously bought themselves a beautiful palazzo on the Grand Canal in Venice, so that retirement was no great hardship to them. The Gregorys would visit them there every spring.

To neither friend did retirement mean inactivity. They continued their work for the National Gallery and their personal picture-collecting, and Sir William continued to gratify what he calls his insatiable appetite for travelling. Three times during his marriage he returned as a visitor to his beloved Ceylon, on the second occasion taking Augusta with him, and giving her a winter in India first. Other winters were spent in Egypt; spring in Spain or Italy, and then on to the Layards. He had, of course, no intention of burying himself at Coole; it was a country house for a few weeks of shooting in the late summer and early autumn. Nor did he take any notice of Dublin, a place of provincial dowdiness to a man of the world like himself, except to give a picture or two to its National Gallery — nothing in comparison with what he did for London's. The tall house in St George's Place, London, was the nearest thing he had to a settled home.

For the Cinderella of Roxborough, it was liberation indeed. It was fulfilment not only as a woman, but as an intelligence. Now at last she had someone to talk to; in fact she had the best company in London to talk to, in the Jane Austen sense of 'the company of clever, well-informed people who have plenty of conversation'. It was frequently the best company in the social sense too; Sir William numbered at least two duchesses among his intimates. 'Freed by my own happy marriage from many family traditions' — so she describes her escape from the Persse conservatism and prejudice. Sir William may not appear much of a revolutionary from our standpoint, but from theirs he was almost as much a rebel and traitor to his class as she was to seem to the next Ascendancy generation. Moreover, he was a great gentleman, with a nation-wide reputation and the grand manner, and if he chose to be a rebel, nobody dared say him nay.

In May of 1881, their son William Robert was born in London, to be the pride of his father's old age, and to his mother the dearest thing on earth.

3

As far as the Galway remove went, only seven miles separated her from Roxborough, but from the first, she says, 'there seemed to be a strangeness and romance about Coole.' And it is not surprising, for the two houses and their demesnes were different worlds. Roxborough was open and windy, bustling and busy, a working estate; Coole was a pleasure-house, a Sleeping Beauty palace in a thick forest. For by his plantations the East India chairman, homesick perhaps for Asia, had created an artificial jungle, quite against the grain of that limestone country. His descendants had inherited his passion for tree-planting. Sir William had turned the nut-wood north of the house into a pinetum, putting, as he cheerfully admits, a great deal of money into the nursery-men's pockets, since many of the rare species of conifer introduced would not take to the limestone, and died. But enough remained to create a handsome sub-Alpine gloom.

The drive was two miles long, and the last mile was first an arching avenue of ilex, then a twisting forest track. The house itself disappointed many (including, years later, Robert Gregory's artist bride) by its architectural poverty. It was an oblong white Georgian building with a plain little porch, the counterpart of hundreds in Ireland. The principal living-rooms, library and drawing-room, looked the other way, west towards the lake, through undistinguished but service-able bays. All the house's distinction lay within.

Four cultivated generations had filled it with books, pictures, statuary, records and mementoes of wide travel, all bearing the imprint of personal taste and personal achievement. It was the house of people who had never been afraid to use their brains.

As at Roxborough, there were rats; indeed, till Robert Gregory married, and his wife persuaded him to pull down the creeper which covered the outer walls, there were rats to a positively embarrassing degree. A visitor of the creeper epoch recalls a rat in her bedroom while she was undressing, a rat inside the mattress when she got into bed, and unmistakeable signs that a rat had been before her when she got down to breakfast next morning; after which she walked the three miles into Gort, and sent herself a telegram, summoning herself home.

Ten minutes' walk along the edge of the paddock at the back of the house brought one out — with a sense of relief if one were of a claustrophobic tendency — on to the edge of a long meandering lake, made even longer in winter by floods, since its waters, like those of the Roxborough river, only reached the sea by an underground channel, which was liable to get blocked. And round the lake lay more vast woods; somewhere in their depths was a perched boulder which when struck emitted musical notes, and could be caused to ring like a chime of church bells. It was all very eerie, and not surprisingly, was a favourite haunt of the Sidhe, those strange Beings, in appearance just like ordinary people until They vanished or filled your pockets with derisory gold, whom it is inadequate and misleading to describe by our English word of Fairies. To the difficulty of finding your way about the woods was added Their propensity for leading you astray, and unwary visitors could be lost for hours, or even a whole night. In later years Their most notable victim was to be Bernard Shaw.

Even in County Galway, the seven miles' removal meant a more intellectual society. Sir William's chief friend in the district was Count de Basterot, a French traveller and littérateur who had inherited an estate on the Burren coast from the Irish side of his family, self-exiled to France in the time of James II. The Count came to Duras for the summer and autumn, much as the Gregorys came to Coole. While the next-door neighbour, at Tullira Castle, was an old-maidish young man named Edward Martyn, heir and hope of one of the rare Catholic landed families. He had literary ambitions which Sir William had encouraged, and was in all directions talented, musically and artistically too. Unfortunately, he was mother-dominated to an extent which made it impossible for him to manage his life or get the full value from his talents. To please his mother, he had Gothicised his house at a cost of £20,000, though besought by Sir William not to. He would do anything to please her but marry, and he lived like a hermit in one of the towers, nourishing a hatred for the rest of womankind. His position as a wealthy and cultivated Catholic later gave him great importance in the Irish Renascence; he became a link between the different sides of the movement; people got to know each other through him, thereafter leaving him behind.

Three years after Lady Gregory's marriage, Dr (later Monsignor) Jerome Fahy was appointed Vicar-General of Gort, the market town nearest to Coole, and this brought into their circle another intelligent man whom as Augusta Persse she would never have been allowed to know. Sir William, it has been noted, was a friend to the Roman Catholic religion, though perhaps not for what Catholics would consider the right reasons. He had always been on good terms with the Bishop and clergy of the Kilmacduagh diocese, and their support had materially assisted his election as member for Galway. And the new Vicar-General was no

ordinary parish priest, but a historian and a man of excep-
tionally enquiring mind.

On the lonely moorland of Kilmacduagh, about three
miles south-west of Gort, he found one of the most considerable groups of ancient ecclesiastical ruins in Ireland: an abbey
church, a monastery, a cathedral, and a well-preserved Round
Tower leaning two feet from the perpendicular. The history
of these monuments had been nearly forgotten, but he made
it his business to 'disinter the buried treasure', as he puts it in
the preface to his *History and Antiquities of the Diocese of
Kilmacduagh*, published in 1893. He is writing, of course, from
the standpoint of his faith, but much of what he 'disinterred'
was folklore, and he was collecting it in the field, a decade
before Lady Gregory and Yeats.

Nor did he limit himself to legends of St Colman, but as
we have seen, brought his story up to date with accounts of
the reigning Ascendancy families; dealing out censure
vigorously, but giving credit to those who had discharged
their responsibilities fairly, particularly to the Gregorys and
the Verekers, the two families who had made Gort such a
well-liking and prosperous little town.

4

The winter spent by the Gregorys in Egypt was an
important one for Augusta, for it was then that, as she puts it,
she 'made her education in politics'. The leaders of the English
colony in Cairo were the Sussex poet and landowner Wilfrid
Scawen Blunt, and his wife Lady Anne, granddaughter of
Byron. Blunt was a great taker-up of causes. He was already
disquieted by British administration in India, and a few years
later, in the Land League troubles, he was to claim the honour
of being the first Englishman to go to gaol for Ireland's sake.
He served a sentence in Galway Gaol for inciting Lord
Clanricarde's tenants to resist eviction, and while this was no

doubt awkward for Sir William Gregory, who was a friend of Lord Clanricarde's, it gave him in Lady Gregory's eyes the status of a hero.

All her life she was fascinated by stories of prisons and prisoners, as indeed anyone with 'rebelly' leanings well may be. From Blunt she learnt what it felt like to be inside the grim gaol at which she had so often stared in awe when her elders came to Galway, and which was to form the background to her two most famous short plays. 'Bereft of books, he found pleasure in watching the seagulls as they hovered overhead, and the jackdaws and sparrows on the lookout for scraps of prison food; talking of horseflesh with the visiting justices, even finding solace in the oakum picking.' Her copy of his prison poems, *In Vinculis*, had as bookmark a piece of tarred rope smuggled from his cell.

His current cause when he met the Gregorys was that of Arabi Bey, an Egyptian officer who had risen by his own abilities from the fellaheen class, and was leading a successful and bloodless revolt against the corruption and incompetence of Turkish rule. The authorities in England regarded him with suspicion, but Blunt had no difficulty in converting the Gregorys to his view that this was a genuine nationalist movement, deserving of support. Sir William proceeded to write a series of letters to *The Times*, of which Blunt says that 'they did much to invest Arabi with that halo of romance which as champion of fellah wrongs was certainly his due'. Unfortunately they also did much to enrage Sir Edward Malet, our Minister in Egypt, who was already pro-Turk, and who saw Blunt and Gregory as busybodies appealing to British public opinion over his head.

When the Gregorys returned to England, it became evident that Sir Edward's counsels were to prevail with Gladstone, and not Sir William's; and Blunt records, significantly, that Sir William grew half-hearted at this setback, but that Lady

Gregory remained staunch, and published a pamphlet in defence of Arabi, which must have been her first printed work.

The British fleet was sent to bombard Alexandria, and for two months Arabi fought a courageous campaign against the might of the British Army. He was then captured and handed over to his enemies, condemned, and would have been hanged, had it not again been for the vigour with which Blunt and the Gregorys stirred the uneasy British conscience. They secured British counsel to defend Arabi at his trial, and raised a fund to pay for it, and it was undoubtedly out of deference to the feeling they aroused that the sentences on Arabi and his associates were commuted to honourable banishment. The place of exile chosen was Ceylon, and they could ensure that he would be received with kindness there.

It was altogether a most instructive episode. The parallel with British treatment of Irish nationalist leaders was not one that could be lost on an intelligent woman. She also learnt how to organise: how to run a campaign, enlist sympathy, raise funds, use influential or wealthy acquaintances, if need be in ways of which they were not fully cognizant. She was to be accused in later years of valuing her title and her position in the county; in fact, she was often socially careless to a fault. But she did value them for the practical results they could achieve. Sir William's intervention in the Arabi affair had shown her that it mattered to bear the famous name of Gregory, that it was something which could be used in a worthy cause. He had put a weapon into her hand.

5

'The landlord-shooting season has set in with great briskness in my county,' Sir William had written to Layard in the autumn of 1881, and he went on to describe the grimmer side of Land League agitation; but in the event, Coole and its inhabitants went unharmed, as they were to do throughout the Black-and-Tan and Civil Wars. At that later date, their immunity was ascribed with bitterness to Lady Gregory's being 'hand in glove with the rebels'. Had she cared to defend herself, she might have reminded her accusers of the tradition that 'Coole was on the side of the people'. It went back further than Augusta Persse.

It is at some point in these Land League years that the undated, 11,000-word essay *An Emigrant's Notebook* (lent to me by her daughter-in-law Mrs Gough) must have been written, for it opens with a description of Roxborough in a state of siege, her brother Algernon and his family guarded by soldiers and police. My guess is that she wrote it in 1884, when Sir William was away on his first visit to Ceylon, and she would be much alone. The word 'emigrant' indicates that she now considers London her principal home.

It is carefully composed, obviously in hope of publication, and the first thing which strikes one is that the cast is that of her plays-to-come. Parents, brothers and sisters scarcely figure, and herself merely as observer. The speaking parts all go to servants and tenants, with Mary Sheridan as leading lady. The story of Mary's own two sickly daughters, and how they were to be brought home from America, constitutes the sort of 'scenario' she would later supply to Hyde.

'. . . the Master, always liberal and desiring that she might end her days happily, gave her money to pay their passage home, and that of her old sister who was with them. Before it had reached New York the news came that the eldest girl had died. That was a sharp grief but not a lasting one, for the younger was her favourite and all her desire centred on the approaching meeting with her. After long waiting there came a telegram from Queenstown saying "Expect us tomorrow". How happy she was! — how excited! — she seemed to have grown young again. In the evening a car drove up to the house and in it was seated, not the daughter, the desire of her heart, the longed and waited for, for she had been laid in her sister's grave in America weeks ago — but the wizened, half-foolish but wholly wideawake old woman, the aunt of the poor dead girls, who had concealed until now the fact that both were dead, lest the passage money should by some means have been taken from her and her old bones not thought worth bringing home.'

Or the story of the gardener's boy and the scullery- maid:

'I do not know that any word of love was spoken between them, but after a time she left, and slanderous tongues began to whisper that she and the handsome garden lad had been too much together. But he when he heard this was very angry, and not being encumbered with much luggage, and having no money to pay for a place in any conveyance, he set out and in two or three days had walked the fifty miles that separated him from the home of the girl whose good name had been tarnished for his sake, however unjustly, and he married her and brought her back his honoured wife. But the neighbours never quite took her to their hearts, or got over her distant birth and that first slander.'

Already she has an ear for the saying that reveals character: for the degrees of snobbery within the peasant hierarchy ('A Sagartin had never condescended to a Callan before'), the honest dignity of a proposal ('Miss, I think myself good enough for you, do you think yourself good enough for me?'), and the ingenious argument of Honest John when reproached for allowing weeds on the drive ('Ah sure, wouldn't it be a quare battle there wouldn't be some soldiers left from!').

I am far from claiming that *An Emigrant's Notebook* is a work of literature. Two things are wrong with it; first, the faint note of condescension, which prevents her doing more than observe her characters from outside, and secondly, the form. What can a series of agreeable anecdotes strung together amount to? — a magazine article or two perhaps, nothing more. It may be for that reason that the manuscript breaks off suddenly; she may have shown it to a publisher, who was discouraging. Like the rest of the Irish Renascence she was waiting for her market, and in the end it was one they had to create for themselves.

No, the importance of the *Notebook* lies not in itself, but in showing her literary personality already in process of formation. When she does become a professional writer, this is the sort of writer she will be, this is the material she will use. She has found it before her meeting with Yeats and Hyde, in a sense before her marriage with Sir William Gregory. Marriage has given her confidence to start writing, but she knows that the world of London dinner-tables, or of European and Asian travels, is of no use to her imagination. That can only expand, and create, in the small green world of Roxborough.

6

As to what she herself was like in her married years, George Moore has left a picture of an earnest, rather priggish young woman, which is unsympathetic but probably not altogether unjust. For one may say they were also her college years; she was making up her deficiencies in education, with Sir William as an urbane and amused tutor. This would be congenial work; what came less easily was the struggle to acquire a social sense. After all it is no light matter to be pitchforked into the best company, when previously one has known no company at all.

'She divided her hair in the middle and wore it smooth on either side of a broad and handsome brow,' Moore writes in *Ave*. 'Her eyes were always full of questions, and her Protestant high-school air became her greatly, and estranged me from her. In her drawing-room were to be met men of assured reputation in literature and politics, and there was always the best reading of the times upon her tables. There was nothing, however, in her conversation to suggest literary facility, and it was a surprise to me to hear one day that she had written a pamphlet in defence of Arabi Pasha, the Egyptian rebel.'

In *Vale* (having in the meantime quarrelled with Yeats), he strengthens the unsympathetic element. 'It was pleasant to pass from her to Sir William, who was more at his ease, more natural. He wore the Lord Palmerston air.' Moore called at the same time as Sir Edwin Arnold, and she invited Sir Edwin to autograph a fan; she did not invite Moore, 'though at that time I had written not only *A Modern Lover*, but also *A Mummer's Wife.* . . . Sir William came into the room just as I was leaving it, and she showed him the fan; he looked a little distressed at her want of tact, and it was some years afterwards that I heard, and not without surprise, that she had shown some literary ability in the editing of his memoirs.' The exquisite non-sequitur of this last sentence will not be lost upon those who relish George Moore and his self-esteem.

But the want of tact is undeniable, and from a relatively inconspicuous fan it later transferred itself to the trunk of a large copper-beech tree by the edge of the lawn at Coole, upon which only those secure of immortality were invited to carve their initials. That 'her visitors' book was a tree' is the only thing many people know about Lady Gregory, and it is often instanced as the supreme monument to her skill as a hostess, whereas in fact it must have been a constant source of social mortification. One can easily picture the mounting chagrin of the not quite sufficiently eminent guest, waiting, penknife at the ready, for the invitation which never came.

It is part of the legend which has built her into a smooth literary hostess, holding the highly-strung poetic group together by miracles of tact and sympathy. It is nonsense, of course. She was a woman primarily concerned, as all talented people must be, with the expression of her own talent. She was a woman with a strong maternal urge, which led her to adopt those she loved as members of her family, so that her house became their home; and to this day their eyes light up when they speak of her and the warmth and ease and protection which she cast around them. But with mere acquaintances, particularly if she sensed in them any antagonism, she could be fumbling and uncertain, sometimes downright clumsy; snubbing when she should have wooed, wooing when she might perhaps have snubbed. And equally to this day, such gaucheries are remembered and held against her. Sir William did much for her, but even he could not turn her — and I do not suppose he could have turned any wife with a spark of literary creativeness — into a real woman of the world.

7

Sir William continued to live his life richly, returning for his last visit to Ceylon in 1890, in the following year starting to read Herodotus 'whom I have not opened since Oxford', and not so completely the reformed character that he could not still relish a little flutter on the turf ('Robert is really beginning to master the very great difficulties of Greek grammar, and I wish I was as sure of Common winning the St Leger on Wednesday . . .'). But by the autumn his health had begun to fail, and his letters to Layard face the end with the courage one would expect. 'I must tell you, as my oldest friend, the whole truth — I am extremely ill. . . . I have very little care for life, but I should like a few years more, to help poor Augusta and Robert, for these are critical times for them.'

He carried on doggedly with his work for the National Gallery, and his insistence on attending the meeting of the Trustees in February 1892 probably hastened his end. Robert, as it happened, was also ill at his preparatory school, and allowed a candle by his bedside. On a night early in March, he woke to find the candle strangely guttering and doubled over, and thought: 'If it falls and goes out, my father will die.' And as he watched, the candle fell.

III

Renascence I: Folklore and Epic

———————

I

'If I had not married I should not have learned the quick enrichment of sentences that one gets in conversation; had I not been widowed I should not have found the detachment of mind, the leisure for observation, necessary to give insight into character, to express and interpret it. Loneliness made me rich — "full", as Bacon says. Company gave me swiftness in putting thought into a word, a sentence.' So she meditates in her *Journals* towards the end of her life.

She was not left a rich woman. Coole, and the rents that still went with it, would pass to Robert when he was of age; it was her business to act as careful steward in the meantime. All she had of her own was her marriage jointure — and what she could earn. Coole must become much more home than it had yet been, and certainly during Robert's school holidays. But equally, she had no intention of returning to the rural imprisonment from which Sir William had rescued her. She meant to keep her place in London literary society, and if possible earn money by her pen.

In November of '92, eight months after Sir William's death, Blunt notes in his diary that his friend Margot Tennant, the future Mrs Asquith, is planning a woman's magazine. 'They are in straits for a political leader-writer, and I suggested Lady Gregory.' The magazine did not materialise, but the suggestion shows her already anxious to be considered a professional writer, with no fine-lady nonsense about amateur status. Later, her enthusiasm for the cause of Irish drama made her improvidently generous about waiving royalties, both at the Abbey and for amateur performances of her plays. But she always saw herself as a professional, and spoke proudly of 'my trade'.

She sold the London house and leased a small flat in Queen Anne's Mansions, and it became a meeting-place between Sir William's friends, people like Lecky and Lyall the historians, James Knowles the architect, Sir Frederick Burton, director of the National Gallery, not to mention 'Duchesses Bedford and St Albans', and the newly-arriving generation, Yeats, 'Fiona' Sharp, Synge, George Moore.

Her own first literary step was to edit and publish the *Autobiography* on which Sir William had been working for the greater part of their married life. She may have helped him with it, but if so, I think it was purely in a secretarial capacity. Its style is essentially masculine and shows no trace of hers.

Next followed *Mr Gregory's Letter Box*, a selection of letters to and from the Under-Secretary, which she found preserved in a large leather box at Coole. It was a task which made much heavier demands on her powers as editor, for it was necessary to link the documents into a coherent story, to fill in character-sketches of the successive Viceroys and Chief Secretaries, and to set the whole against the struggle for Catholic Emancipation, to which old Mr Gregory (unlike his grandson) was opposed. She has done the work with ease and grace, and it is still extremely readable. The prologue shows her capable of a neat Jane Austen parody, and the second chapter has her first *trouvaille* in the way of living folk-history, a peasant account of Daniel O'Connell's birth as 'the gift of God'. Her final verdict on the Under-Secretary and his masters is that they were 'all, all honourable men, and not only that, but truly anxious for the welfare of their country,

The Autograph Tree: a Bord Failte photograph taken in 1927. Synge's is the lyre-like cipher top right, with Shaw's 'G.B.S.' below it. Yeats and O'Casey are easily made out. The initials of J.B. and Jack B. Yeats are round to the left, and AE's colophon is enclosed by a triangle. Lady Gregory's I.A.G. and her son's W.R.G. are in the centre, but the 'E.M.M.' above them cannot be Martyn, as his middle name was Joseph.

looking with kindly, if somewhat prejudiced, eyes through their parti-coloured glasses'.

Nevertheless, in *Our Irish Theatre* she says it was the historical reading needed for this book that turned her into a Home Ruler. 'I defy anyone to study Irish history without getting a dislike and distrust of England.' She might more truly have said that it completed the process begun in the nursery at Roxborough, and intensified by the Arabi campaign. But it seems probable that she was unwilling to break completely with Sir William's policy during his lifetime, though one of his letters to Layard suggests that they disagreed amicably over Parnell.

The *Letter Box* was not published till 1898, so that work on it must have continued during her first 'renascence' years.

Sir Henry Layard survived his friend by two years, and thereafter the link between the widows became, if possible, even closer. Their situations were in some ways alike, for both had married men much older than themselves, and Enid Layard had literary antecedents and sympathies, even if she had no creative ambition of her own. Her mother was the remarkable Lady Charlotte Guest, wife of the great Welsh ironmaster and 'richest manufacturer in the world', and translator of the *Mabinogion*, the Welsh Arthurian legends — translations which formed the basis for several of Tennyson's *Idylls of the King*. Indeed, Lady Layard's Christian name was taken from the heroine of the epic's most popular episode. Lady Charlotte's fascinating *Diaries* make it appear highly likely that Layard had been in love with her, and had remained a bachelor for her sake, until he married her daughter in late middle-age.

Lady Gregory continued to pay regular spring visits to her friend at the palazzo on the Grand Canal; in return Lady Layard came to Coole in the summer, and sometimes the

D

friends would rent rooms at the Beach House on the Burren coast. The typewriter which was to make so much literary history, and which in its exhausted old age was to require so much tinkering at the hands of her Sapper grandson, was a gift from Lady Layard, as well as 'the great gift of her friendship through more than half my life'.

Enid Layard died in 1913, just as the first great Abbey epoch was ending. If the letters of Lady Gregory to this intelligent and understanding woman are ever discovered, they should throw a revealing light, not only on her own development, but on the whole dramatic movement.

Visitors to Coole were not only the distinguished. She adored children, and delighted to fill the house with Robert's school friends, and with Persse nephews and nieces, who, as might have been expected from so large a clan, were numerous, and sometimes impecunious. And at Christmas and in the summer, wagonette-loads of children were brought in from the Workhouse, which was also the orphanage, for lavish parties, with a present for every child at Christmas, sports and donkey-rides in the summer; the hostess rolling up her sleeves and labouring as hard as her modest domestic staff.

This Gort Workhouse deserves a word to itself, for in it she collected much of her folklore and at least one of her plots for plays. It was far from being the grim institution we in England associate with the word, but on the contrary an ancient and beautiful foundation comprising hospital, orphanage and old people's home, and forming a real centre of social service for the town. Even before Lady Gregory's death it was dispersed, her voice being one of the few raised in protest, and the buildings, all but the Master's house, pulled down. Old people in Gort who have no one to care for them must now end their days in Galway, far from the scenes and faces they know. It is their loss, and the town's.

An essential element was added to her literary equipment some two years after Sir William's death; at last she succeeded in learning Irish. The final impetus came from Robert, who had followed in his father's footsteps by taking a classical scholarship to Harrow, and in the summer holidays had the creditable impulse 'to learn a nearer language'. Martyn at Tullira was asked to recommend a teacher, but recommended instead the Irish Grammar of Father O'Growney and lent them a fine old Irish Bible, and with these mother and son taught themselves. She had a natural gift for languages, but it was too late in life for her to become anything of an Irish scholar, and she always regretted it. There was no question of her either writing in modern Irish, or being able to read ancient Irish. But she learnt enough for her purposes; she could follow a conversation, ask questions, read a modern text, and translate accurately from it into English. If injudicious admirers ever claimed more for her, it was not her fault.

There is a final point of some psychological significance to be made about Lady Gregory in these early years of her widowhood, her choice of dress. She went into mourning for Sir William, and she never came out of it. 'Such a pity she had to choose to dress like Queen Victoria', people have said, and her small stature and increasing plumpness heightened the resemblance. Certainly she was no admirer of the Famine Queen, and could have had no notion of imitating her, but both were widows, and both wore the rigidly conventional garments of the time. To the end of her life she was draped from head to foot in voluminous black; elegant in the eyes of her friends, stuffy and dowdy according to her enemies, but in any case, one would think, hot and inconvenient for a woman who was so active in all directions, including forestry and gardening.

What was her reason? She was only forty when he died,

and still attractive, and could presumably have married again had she wished. It seems to me a subconscious indication that she did not wish. A similar hauling-down of the flag of sex may be noted in the lives of other women unusually gifted: in Jane Austen, for instance, taking to caps in her thirties, or in George Eliot, whose eminently respectable liaison with Lewes could not tempt her into any frivolity of appearance. It is their way of silencing — or at any rate, of hoping to silence — the tongues of gossip and speculation; of signalling their resolve to concentrate on the work which, as it seems to them, they were born to do.

2

Why an Irish Renascence? — why at that time, in that way? The explanation given by both Yeats and Lady Gregory, and repeated by historians after them, is that the nationalist urge, disappointed by the overthrow of Parnell, converted itself into an imaginative and creative urge; that people turned to art and literature because they were sickened of politics. 'With the passing away of Parnell's long dominance, his necessary discipline,' she says in her *Hugh Lane's Life and Achievement*, 'there had come a setting loose of the mind, of the imagination, that had for so long dwelt upon some battle at Westminster or some disputed farm.'

There is a truth here, but like most convenient explanations it is not more than a half-truth. To take the leaders alone, it is just possible to picture Lady Gregory as a Member of Parliament, though she would have been driven to it by her social-worker conscience rather than by any real liking for the trade. But can we seriously believe that the brooding lyric genius of Yeats, the totally non-political outlook of Synge, the violently anti-political temperament of Douglas Hyde, would have been deflected from their courses by the return of the Irish Parliament to College Green?

My own suspicion is that any large-scale creative movement is a matter of luck. The people with talents, and with the sort of talents that can influence each other, happen to coincide in time and space. In Ireland, they also happened to be in time to catch the last flickers of a dying language, and the far from dying traditions of a strong folk-culture and memory; and the researches of scholars immediately preceding them had brought to light an ancient literature which would be an inspiration and starting-point. I believe that it would all have happened in much the same way had there been no political vacuum. And in fact, those of them whose real bent was for politics — Arthur Griffith, for example, or Maud Gonne — never formed an integral part of the Renascence, and quickly came to regard it with hatred, as something that deflected energy and got in their way.

At all events, the starting-point for Lady Gregory, and for many like her, was the publication in 1893 of two books, W. B. Yeats's *The Celtic Twilight* and Douglas Hyde's *Love Songs of Connacht*. And modest acorns indeed they are to have given birth to such a tree, the sort of shabby little volumes you would expect to pick up on a bookstall for sixpence. Lacking her early diaries, I cannot tell how soon after their publication she read them.

The Celtic Twilight in its original edition of 1893 is a slight book, chiefly a reprint of Yeats's articles in the *National Observer*, and dealing with his subjective experiences quite as much as with the folklore he gathered. But the opening chapters, on old Paddy Flynn the Sligo story-teller of his boyhood, at once took her mind back to Mary Sheridan, and set her reflecting that there must be equally productive seers and storytellers in Galway. Well before she met him, she had begun to look for news of the invisible world, 'for his stories were of Sligo and I felt jealous for Galway,' she says in the introduction to *Visions and Beliefs*. 'This beginning of knowledge was a great excitement for me, for though I had heard all my life some talk of the faeries and the banshee (having indeed some reason to believe in this last), I had never thought of giving heed to what I, in common with my class, looked on as fancy or superstition. It was certainly because of this unbelief that I had been told so little about them.'

The *Love Songs of Connacht* is, from the folklore point of view, a very different matter. It is the work of a man who, although Anglo-Irish like Lady Gregory herself, had contrived to learn Irish in his boyhood, and to assimilate it so completely that he wrote and spoke in it better than he did in English. He became a vernacular poet of the first order, whose songs passed into folk-culture in his lifetime. He had taken not only the peasant speech but something of the peasant outlook upon himself, and seemed to them almost a reincarnation of Blind Raftery, their last great wandering poet, who had died sixty years before.

The *Love Songs*, however, are all traditional poems he had collected, with translations. Some of these are in verse (one of them, 'My Grief on the Sea', has achieved something like fame through its inclusion in *The Oxford Book of English Verse*), but more important are the literal prose translations. They are really intended as a sort of 'crib', to help the student of Irish, and are frequently relegated to a footnote. But seldom can a book's footnotes have made so much literary history before.

To one like Lady Gregory, whose ear was already attuned to Galway folk-speech, this strange-looking prose was immediately recognisable. It was the English of people who were mentally translating from the Gaelic, or at any rate whose recent ancestors had done so. Her own new-found Irish gave her the clue to a right appreciation of the lilting music she had heard all her life; a tune that would go like this:

'My plough is to cease, And my lea-land to sow, And all that is to be done, Me to be out, In rain and frost, In hope that you would give me liking.'

Or like this:

'This weariness and grief, Are going greatly, greatly round my heart, And the full of my two shoes of it, And the tears dropping down with me. It is what I think the Sunday long from me, Oh, thousand treasures, till you pass the way. And my darling twice over you are, Giving farewell to you, Until I return.'

The content is often as touching as the words are beautiful, and Hyde himself notes a curious fact about these love-laments, that the greater part of them are, or purport to be, by women. The girl mourns her lover departed, to the hill, or to America. She never loses him to another woman; she simply loses him.

Between them, these two books provided the revelation Lady Gregory had been obscurely seeking for herself. From the *Twilight* she learnt that the folklore tradition was not dead, and from the *Love Songs* that the lyrical tradition was not dead either, 'and it does not comfort me', she says, 'to think how many besides myself, having spent a lifetime in Ireland, must make this confession.'

But it was not too late to profit by it. 'This discovery, this disclosure of the folk-learning, the folk-poetry, was the small beginning of a weighty change. It was an upsetting of the table of values, an astonishing excitement. The imagination of Ireland had found a new homing-place. My own imagination was aroused. I was becoming conscious of a world close to me and that I had been ignorant of. It was not now in the corners of newspapers I looked for poetic emotion, nor even to the singers in the streets. It was among the farmers and potato diggers and old men in workhouses and beggars at my own door that I found what was beyond these, and yet farther beyond that drawing-room poet of my childhood

[Moore] in the expression of love, and grief, and the pain of parting, that are the disclosure of the individual soul.'*

But I would still emphasise that her 'discovery' differs from Yeats's and Synge's, in that it is not primarily new knowledge, but a new attitude to what she knew already. She had lived among the people all her life, nearly as intimately as Hyde, and her first attempts at writing prove that she already understood they were to be her material. But she had known them from without, as an improver, a social worker, a daughter of the Big House. Now she was to start all over again, going to them as learner, not as teacher. Now she would believe; not of course actually in the Sidhe, but in the reality and dignity of the native poetic tradition. And so she could get them to talk to her; literally in their own language in the case of old people who knew only Irish, but what was even more important, in the language of minds akin.

3

The next step was to meet her heroes, and their followers who were thinking along the same lines as herself. As a woman, as a late-Victorian Irish county lady, she could not

* From the Preface to the *Kiltartan Poetry Book.*
She must certainly also have read Hyde's earlier book, *Beside the Fire,* though I have not found a specific mention of it. This appeared in 1890 and is a collection of prose folk-stories, with translations. In its most interesting preface, Hyde first castigates the unscientific approach and 'embroidery' of his pre-decessors, then describes his own way of handling the old people and getting their stories from them. 'Half a glass of Ishka-baha, a pipe of tobacco, and a story of one's own are the best things to begin with. If, however, you start to take down the story verbatim, as an unwary collector might do, you destroy all, or your shanachie becomes irritable. . . . What you must generally do is to sit quietly smoking your pipe, without the slightest interruption, not even when he comes to words and phrases which you do not understand.' Finally, he explains his principle of translation; he has used many idioms based on Gaelic, 'but only of the kind used all over Ireland, the kind people themselves use.' In the dialogue of the stories there are many of the turns of speech one particularly associates with Lady Gregory's 'Kiltartan' dialect: for example, on page 97, the use of the 'Kiltartan infinitive': 'It's a great shame, you to be coming back again, after being seven days in your grave.'

go into the clubs and bars of that man's country, where the movement was being made. As a matter of fact, she would find it difficult to do so today. They must be inveigled into coming to her, either in London or at Coole. The significance of Coole in her development has not, I think, been properly appreciated. It was not a free poets' hotel which she ran as a sort of literary social-climber. It was her principal opportunity of sharing in what was going on.

Yeats says she had met him briefly at some literary function in London; if so it was probably in 1895. The next year, he and his friend Arthur Symons took the Irish walking-tour which was to have such momentous consequences. They stayed for a while with Edward Martyn at Tullira, and while they were there she called. Did Martyn invite her, or did instinct tell her that this was the moment? Relations between the houses were friendly, as the incident of the Irish Bible shows, and he probably sent her word. Later on he grew jealous of her, and felt that she had stolen his friends; though in truth it was his own increasing eccentricity that made Tullira a less pleasant house to stay in than Coole.

She invited Yeats and Symons to lunch; then, after Symons had gone back to London, she invited Yeats for a short stay. When she went to her London flat for the winter they saw more of each other, and he told her that he had written a play, *The Countess Cathleen*, on a mediaeval Irish theme, but could find no one to produce it. He wanted to take a little theatre somewhere in the suburbs and produce it himself, but he had no money. Though he was already recognised as a major poet, though his polemical gifts and his founding of the London and Dublin Irish Literary Societies had made him the acknowledged leader of the revival, he was still a desperately poor man, who hardly knew where his next five pounds was to come from — sometimes not even his next five shillings.

Later on, her physical care and cosseting of Yeats were to

provoke titters, and certainly they must have been aggra-
vating to fellow-guests, not to mention her own family. But
it must not be forgotten that in the first years of his visits to
Coole, he really was in need of rest and good food and fresh
air, quite as much as of assistance in his literary projects, and
of sympathy in his infatuation with the lovely revolutionary,
Maud Gonne.

His first long visit was in the summer of 1897, but before it
he spent a month at Tullira, and it must have been during
that time that the famous meeting at Count de Basterot's
house, from which is usually dated the 'founding of the
National Theatre', took place. Lady Gregory says she was
staying for a few days with the Count, when Martyn brought
Yeats over to lunch. Her memory for events is honest and
reliable, but she admits somewhere that using it so much in
folklore-collecting has weakened 'that useful and practical
side that is concerned with names and dates and the multipli-
cation table, and the numbers of friends' houses in a street'.
In her account of the meeting in *Our Irish Theatre*, she is a
year too late.

It was wet, and they talked again of the theatre project.
Yeats still hankered after London, Martyn, who also had a
play ready, after Germany; it was she who, although she had
never been particularly interested in theatrical matters,
suggested that the proper place to give Irish plays in was
Dublin. And probably it was she who, remembering how
money was raised to defend Arabi, proposed that it should be
raised for this cause also, by appealing to their friends for
guarantees.

As they talked, 'things seemed to grow possible.' They
would take a Dublin theatre and bring over English actors;
there was no question of using Irish actors since there were no
Irish actors, so far as anybody knew; Dublin's theatre-going
was catered for by visiting English companies. And Irishmen,

whether actual or impersonated, were always presented on the stage as figures of farce.

When Yeats came to Coole to begin his stay with her, they wrote their letter of appeal on the typewriter, which was still a new toy. The response, from a list which varied between Sir William's august friends and the old Fenian leader John O'Leary, was warm and encouraging, and the plays were given two years later, though in the event the guarantors did not have to pay up, since Martyn bore the expenses of the production himself.

To the rest of the theatre story, I will return in the next chapter. Lady Gregory's part in it in these first years was that of organiser and hostess. Her literary work was being done in folklore, which is my present concern.

'Finding that I could not work,' says Yeats in *Dramatis Personae*, 'and thinking the open air salutary, Lady Gregory brought me from cottage to cottage collecting folklore.' This has been solemnly interpreted to mean that Lady Gregory took up folklore-collecting for the benefit of Yeats' health; but of course folklore was her new and chief interest before he appeared personally on the scene. Yeats knew the country people of his native Sligo, but a good part of his childhood had been spent in England, and in any case the local accent varies as widely in Ireland as it does here. The Gregory family assure me that he had considerable difficulty in understanding the Galway peasantry when they spoke. If George Moore is to be believed — and after all his account in *Ave* was accepted by Yeats and Lady Gregory as on the whole a fair picture of their relationship and activities — he did not try very hard. 'She goes into the cottage and listens to the story, takes it down, while you wait outside, sitting on a bit of wall, Yeats, like an old jackdaw, and then filching her manuscript to put style upon it, just as you want to put style on me.'

(Incidentally, Yeats's sacerdotal black clothes caused him

to be mistaken for a missioner when they went further afield, into districts where Lady Gregory was not known by reputation; and a Clare confrère appealed in alarm to Dr Fahy, who told him roundly not to be a fool.)

An extension of the legend insists that she invited Yeats's fellow-authors to Coole in order to amuse him, and that they only came because he was the attraction. She invited them for their own sakes — and hers — because each of them had something to give her. And if at first some came because he would be there, it is equally arguable that for the same reason they later stayed away. The superb polemical authority which made Yeats the fighting leader of the movement was also bound, as time went on, to alienate those of his contemporaries who considered themselves his intellectual equals. His following was mainly among women, and the young.

He certainly did not lack for sympathetic women friends, but the summer of 1897 established Lady Gregory as the one with whom he felt the closest intellectual kinship, and her house and woods and lake as the spot that was to be more precious in inspiration to him than anywhere else on earth. For the rest of her life she would have the happiness of watching his genius flower there, and of reading in his own hand, never first in print, the poems he composed as he paced the long walk between lawn and flower-border, or the strange brown-velvet moss of the lake's shores, arriving at his famous count of 'nine and fifty swans'. It was a link that nothing would break till the woman, and the house itself, died.

4

Was she in love with him? The question crops up with such dreary regularity whenever the names of Yeats and Lady Gregory are mentioned (or for that matter, the names of Yeats and any of his numerous women friends) that her biographer cannot conscientiously avoid it.

There were only thirteen years between them, and no amount of widow's weeds can ever quite silence gossip, particularly not Irish country gossip. There were jokes made about 'Lady Yeats' in Galway county circles, already piqued by her neglect. And then after her death, further titillation was provided by the irresistibly racy and amusing memoirs of Maud Gonne, *A Servant of the Queen*. There was a joyous pouncing on the passage which reads:

'I had been much amused in Dublin watching the rivalry between Lady Gregory and a rich English woman, Miss Horniman; both were interested in Willie and both were interested in the theatre. Miss Horniman had the money and was willing to spend it, but Lady Gregory had the brains. They should have been allies, for both stood for art for art's sake and deprecated the intrusion of politics, which meant Irish freedom; instead they were rivals, they both liked Willie too well. Lady Gregory won the battle. . . .'

But even from this short quotation it will be evident that Miss Gonne is not an unbiassed observer. She was a natural and instinctive revolutionary, and like all her kind, lacked a strict regard for truth. Any insinuation was allowable as long as it served the Cause. Her description of Lady Gregory at their first meeting gives sufficient taste of her reliability — 'a queer little old lady, rather like Queen Victoria.' Not even the widow's weeds can make that an accurate picture of a woman still under fifty, by one who would not herself see thirty again.

Maud Gonne has one object in view; she is out to make Lady Gregory and Miss Horniman look ridiculous. Her admirer having written one propaganda play in which she had scored an immense success, she was avid for more, and in her view they had deflected his genius from 'Irish freedom' to 'art for art's sake'. What better revenge than to depict them as two elderly women fruitlessly sighing for a handsome poet, whose affections she was so comfortably certain of possessing herself?

If any speculation is permissible on the unwritten feelings of the dead, then perhaps I too may be allowed to speculate that, at this stage, nobody was in love with Yeats; not even poor Miss Horniman, who is credited with founding the Gaiety in Manchester for love of the theatre, but not the Abbey in Dublin for the same reason. Maud Gonne certainly was not physically attracted by him, or she would have married him despite the fine talk about remaining single for Ireland's sake. When she did find a man to whom she was so attracted, she married him against the advice of his friends and hers, and regretted it forthwith. Is it not possible that Yeats had the traditional poet's following of twenty lovesick maidens playing archaic musical instruments (Florence Farr with her psaltery is a figure straight from *Patience*), but that in the event 'nobody was Bunthorne's bride'?

What is plain from his correspondence is that Yeats was one of those rare men who have a gift for intellectual friendship with women, and with several of them simultaneously. In his company, they enjoyed the stimulus of that wide-ranging conversation, and in absence, a flow of exciting if not always very legible letters, which took them right into the workshop of genius, and were not without a leaven of sardonic humour and sometimes even of agreeable scandal.

It was a privilege they knew how to value. The friendships survived his correspondents' marriages, and eventually his own, surely another pointer to their nature. True, he lost Miss Horniman, but there the split was for reasons of artistic policy, not of sentiment.

In the case of Lady Gregory, I see no reason to suppose that the relationship was other in spirit than what Mrs Asquith took it to be in fact, that of aunt to nephew. She was a young aunt to John Shawe-Taylor and Hugh Lane, an only slightly younger one to Yeats. Her link with him was closer, because their common interest was literature, which she practised; with the other two it was politics and art, in which she was not so immediately involved. In her letters he is 'My dear Willie', but in his she is always 'My dear Lady Gregory'; he never addressed her by her Christian name.

And from the works of any writer of fiction, it is possible to deduce the ideal of an attractive mate. It is not easy in Lady Gregory's case, because she deals so little with romantic love, but the composite picture that emerges is something very simply and directly masculine, combining the *grand seigneur* urbanity of Sir William with the physical dash and prowess of the Persse brothers; nothing in the least like Yeats.

It seems to me credible that after Sir William's death, she found her emotional outlet in her son Robert, and her intellectual outlet in her work and in her friendships, particularly with Yeats. She no longer looked to find them in the same person. And if she had her moments of frustration, there is certainly no hint of it in her autobiographical writings. On the contrary, she had made for herself, largely by her own initiative, a position more interesting than that of any other woman in Ireland, and her recollections breathe a continual astonished thankfulness at her great good luck.

5

It was also through the invaluable Edward Martyn that she met Douglas Hyde. She was lunching at Tullira when he came in with a broken bicycle, having been searching the neighbourhood for memories of the blind poet, Raftery. She does not give the date of this meeting, but I think it must have been in the summer of 1898. He first stayed at Coole that winter for a shooting party, for he was a great sportsman.

She found him, as everyone did, an immediately captivating personality; a big genial man, with a walrus moustache, who could go into castle or cottage on terms of complete equality, help the woman of the house at her churning, or take the baby on his knee. He had his Gaelic nickname, An Craoibhin Aoibhin, the Sweet Little Branch — his portrait by Sarah Purser shows him holding a branch with golden apples — but in Dublin he was 'Duggie', and is still, in spite of his later presidential honours, affectionately so remembered.

He was utterly modest about his own writing; the aim of his life, to which his poetic gift was made subservient, was to keep Irish alive and spread it as a spoken language, and to revive it as a written one. If Yeats was the movement's literary leader, Hyde was its standard-bearer on the linguistic and social flanks. His Gaelic League, founded in the same year that he published the *Love Songs*, was a nation-wide effort to promote the study of Irish; but as well as classes and lectures, to which men and women went eagerly after the day's work, it also developed a sort of Women's Institute side in the country districts, with open-air excursions and outings, games and competitions, and gatherings for a local Feis, rather on the model of the Welsh Eisteddfod. And this filled a very real want, for as a result of Land League bitterness the Big House had largely abdicated as a centre of social life.

The movement was to be non-political; Hyde insisted, with something like passion, on that. It was to be open to everyone, even Orangemen, in the unlikely event of any wishing to join. Poor man, he might as well have hoped to turn the River Shannon back in its bed. The Gaelic League was in its essence, as a modern critic has well said, a sublimated separatist movement. No sooner did a Unionist come into contact with it than his Unionism began to weaken, and Sinn Fein would not find the slightest difficulty in infiltrating into it in due course, thereby nearly breaking its founder's heart. But that was far away. These were the sunny days of the League's first joyous enthusiasm, when the pretty girls at the Galway Feis wore An Craoibhin's name embroidered round their hats.

Douglas Hyde in 1898, from a drawing by J. B. Yeats the Elder.
Reproduced by courtesy of the National Gallery of Ireland.

Galway already had its branch. At Christmas, Hyde and his associate in language teaching, Miss Borthwick, put on a Punch and Judy show at the school feast in Coole, which Lady Gregory proudly claims as the beginning of modern Irish drama, 'and the delighted children went back to tell their parents what grand curses An Craoibhin had put on the baby and the policeman.' On January 8th was formed the Kiltartan branch, Kiltartan being the name of the district in which Coole stands, and also of the hamlet, scarcely more than a scattering of cottages and the Gregory-built school, at the crossroads outside its gates.

Dr Fahy presided, and dwelt on the fact that though the use of Irish would not help anyone's material prospects, still there were things more important than wealth, and the loss of their native tongue meant the loss of independence of thought and character. He thanked Lady Gregory for the encouragement she had given to the language, and there was a special word of praise for Robert for taking it up in addition to his school work. Hyde made his usual winning speech; then Lady Gregory urged the teaching of real Irish songs; she had heard a man when asked for one oblige with the Cockney music-hall ditty 'Where did you get that hat, where did you get that tile?' A secretary was elected, and said that all there understood Irish and most spoke it. Now they would learn to read and write it too.

6

Having Hyde to share the folklore-collecting round must have been an enchanting as well as an instructive experience, but though she could never hope to identify herself so completely with the people as he did, though she would remain 'Your Ladyship' and never have a Gaelic name, she had already evolved her own fully effective technique. This is confirmed to me by eighty-two-year-old Paudeen Coneely

E

of Inishmaan, the middle one of the Aran Islands, who remembers quite clearly her visit in the summer of 1898.

She had started collecting on the Burren coast of Galway Bay, where the family went regularly for its breath of sea air; then moved out to the Aran Islands, where her visit coincided with Synge's first one. On the main island of Inishmore, she saw him in the distance, but 'I was jealous of not being alone on the island among the fishers and sea-weed gatherers. I did not speak to the stranger, nor was he inclined to speak to me. He also looked on me as an intruder.'

Like Synge, but apparently even more rapidly, she decided that Inishmore was too sophisticated for her purpose, and moved across to Inishmaan. Here she found an almost untouched peasant culture: the men wearing suits of donkey-grey homespun, belted by the brightly woven *crois*, the magnificently tall and handsome women in red petticoats (a deep rose-madder which is most beautiful against the pinkish-grey limestone of which the island is composed), the small fry of both sexes in skirts that made them look like miniature choirboys. Miraculously, and with a little judicious cosseting by the Irish Government, this culture survives yet, and it is possible to see and hear what Synge and Lady Gregory saw and heard, including the Irish of people most of whom have no English worth mentioning.

Visitors of the lady class on Inishmaan were rare, and she has stayed in Paudeen's mind as 'a very simple, easy lady, with no airs to her at all'. He was struck by the good Irish she had, so that she could go among the people and get their stories, whereas Mr Synge had no Irish at all, and could only talk to those islanders, like young Martin MacDonough, whose English was reasonably good.

In fact, Synge's academic Irish was probably better than Lady Gregory's, but he had no facility in the spoken language, and in any case was chiefly interested in Anglo-Irish habits of speech; nor was he primarily a collector of folklore. But Lady Gregory was, and she spent most of her time in the cottages talking to the old people, who still believed in fairies and hauntings. Among the young men of Paudeen's generation scepticism was already setting in, though as far as story-telling goes, he himself in his later years has become the most renowned shanachie on the island.

She stayed, like Synge after her, in the MacDonough cottage at the foot of Dun Conor, the only one then having an extra bedroom and so able to receive visitors. In *Visions and Beliefs* she describes a typical evening in the kitchen there, 'when the fishers had come home and had eaten, and the fire was stirred and flashed on the dried mackerel and conger eels hanging over the wide hearth, and the little vessel of cod-oil had a fresh wick put in it and lighted. The men would sit in a half-circle on the floor, passing the lighted pipe from one to another; the women would find some work with yarn or wheel.' She would not find much change today. The room keeps the 'beauty and distinction' that delighted Synge; like all Aran kitchens it is open to the rafters, and with its white-washed walls and deep hearth gives a sense of spaciousness; the turf fire burns still, and the present Mrs MacDonough and her daughter in their red dresses sit on stools one each side of it, with their children and grandchildren grouped around them. Bottled gas has replaced the cod-oil lamp, and the wool is sent to the mainland to be spun in a factory, but it comes back again to the knitters, and 'work with yarn' has carried the fame of Aran jerseys far across the seas.

But the Burren coast and the islands had no monopoly of folklore; she soon found there was plenty of unharvested material nearer home, and that Coole itself was an excep-tionally haunted place, with quite a body of legend gathered round it. It is now that Shamrock and the phaeton come into their glory. They took her on expeditions over the hills, sometimes with Yeats or Hyde, more often alone. ('A bad-tempered pony' is how a niece remembers Shammy, but he was old by then, and perhaps felt himself entitled to fits of temperament.)

She identified Raftery's grave in Killeenan churchyard, from an old man who had helped to dig it as a boy, and she arranged that a stone should be cut and put up. 'And as I went back along the silent road,' she tells us in *Poets and Dreamers*, the first of her folklore books, 'there was suddenly a sound of horses and a rushing and waving about me, and I found myself in the midst of the County Galway Foxhounds, come back from cub-hunting. The English M.F.H. and his wife rode by, and I wondered if they had ever heard of the poet whose last road this had been. Most likely not, for it is only among the people that his name has been kept in remembrance.' Already she and the English M.F.H. were living in different worlds.

Hyde seems to have committed to her the care of Raftery's reputation; her own prize exhibit, so to speak, was a Clare wise woman and healer named Biddy Early, round whom legend had gathered so thickly that, in that country of sparse communications, no one quite knew whether she were alive or dead. Her home had been at Tulla on the other side of Slieve Echtge, and reaching it involved first spending a night at Chevy Chase of the girlhood shooting parties, and then driving 'eight strong miles over the mountain. It was a wild road, and the pony had to splash his way through two unbridged rivers, swollen with the summer rains. The red mud of the roads, the purple heather and foxglove, the brown bogs were a contrast to the grey rocks and walls. . . .' She found the cottage, and learnt that Biddy had died some twenty years before, but was shown the shed where she would confer with her invisible friends — for the ills she cured were those caused by the 'touch' of the Sidhe, chiefly, it would appear, arthritis of the hip. Yeats consulted a living healer about his eyesight, but the trouble was not of sheoguy origin, and nothing could be done.

Like most seekers after the supernatural, Lady Gregory generally found herself a generation too late. The same fate had befallen Dr Johnson in his quest for possessors of the Second Sight in the Hebrides. But an old woman of Kiltartan was still in regular communication with Them, and was able to inform her that 'Coole is alive with Them, as plenty as grass. In May they are as thick everywhere as the grass, but there's no fear at all for you or for Master Robert. I know that, for *one* told it to me.'

Treat Them civilly and They would treat you civilly — that seemed to be the safe maxim for dwelling in a thickly sheoguy demesne. Never harm the creatures that were under Their special protection. 'Bid Master Robert never to shoot a hare, for you wouldn't know what might be in it.' Weasels and seals were similarly sheoguy, and also old tom-cats, 'there's some that have heard them together at night talking Irish.' Never interfere with the raths and forths (the pre-historic camps and barrows) that are Their dwellings. 'There was an engineer here when the road was being made, a sort of idolator or a foreigner he was — anyway he made it through the forth, and he didn't live long after. Those other engineers, beyond at Ardrahan when the railway was made, I'm told they avoided such things.'

(And while I was collecting material for this book, labourers in County Mayo refused to build a fence through the centre of a rath, and made the front pages of the Irish papers.)

The Sidhe were everywhere, they emigrated with their hosts and victims; they were to be found in the back streets of Manchester and London, and were thick on the ground in Boston and New York. 'There's no doubt at all but that there's the same sort of things in other countries,' a miller summed it up, 'but you hear more about them in these parts, because the Irish do be more familiar in talking of them.'

And so on through the 600-odd pages of the two-volume *Visions and Beliefs in the West of Ireland*, her final compendium of folklore. It was not published till 1920, but the main research for it was done in these pre-theatre years. Her account of her personal adventures in collecting adds greatly to the book's charm, but the actual stories are presented with complete objectivity. Never does it occur to the reader to ask: Does Lady Gregory believe this? He simply registers: This is what she must have been told. It is the modern scientific attitude, at the opposite pole from Yeats's questings after 'proof'.

The mother of folklore — so Dr Thomas Wall of the Irish Folklore Commission has called her, and he finds in her a reliability which made her almost a human tape-recorder. And in fact her modern successor, the Commission's Galway field researcher, does not use a tape-recorder. His equipment is still what she listed as hers, patience, reverence, and a good memory.

7

Alongside folklore was the folk-learning, poems and stories handed down orally. ('I never saw a man that could read an open book, was able to tell a story out of the mouth,' a proud illiterate said.) The poets ranged from Raftery of the day before yesterday to Cuchulain's bard of remotest times. She would speak a verse from one of Hyde's *Love Songs*, and an old man or woman would take up the rest, often in a different version, sometimes in a more beautiful one. But love-songs were not the favourites. 'Love of country is, I think, the real passion; and bound up with it are love of home, of family, love of God. Constancy and affection in marriage are the rule, but marriage "for love" is all but unknown; marriage is a matter of commonsense arrangement between the heads of families.'

The epics she was puzzling out in scholarly translations from ancient texts lived on in the folk memory. A centenarian told her how Cuchulain fought with and slew his own son; others could describe the actual physical appearance of Deirdre, and of Grania who was to mean so much to her. 'Grania was very small, only four feet.'

And the special branch of folk-learning which she might almost claim as her discovery was folk-history, the 'Alfred and the cakes' sort of history which shocks the professional historian by its flagrant divergence from fact, yet which has survived because it embodies an element of symbolic truth. For example, the picture the folk-memory kept of the greatest Tudor: 'Queen Elizabeth was awful. Beyond everything she was. When she came to the turn she dyed her hair red, and whatever man she had to do with, she would send him to the block in the morning, that he would be able to tell nothing.' Folk-history was made under one's eyes, weaving itself round the recently dead like O'Connell and Biddy Early, and even round the living.

She was told of Queen Victoria: 'It is when she was a girl she put on clothes like your own — lady's clothes — and she went to the Pope. Did she turn Catholic? She'd be beheaded if she did; the Government would behead her; it is the Government has power in England.'

8

In 1900 a Commission was appointed to enquire into secondary education in Ireland, largely through Hyde's agitation to have Irish included in the curriculum. It was the signal for the pundits of Trinity College to come out virulently against both language and literature. 'All folklore is at bottom abominable,' the Commission was told.

The Gaelic League were furious, and Yeats was invited to make an English translation which should reveal the poetry and dignity of the Irish epics, but he could not spare the time from his own work, and Lady Gregory offered to supply the want. 'I hesitated,' he says, 'I saw nothing in her past to fit her for the work.' Why not, when there was the *Letter Box* to prove that she could turn a collection of documents into a coherent story, and all those thousands of words of folklore transcribed from the people under his very nose?

But Augusta Persse of Roxborough had not grown up expecting encouragement, and her own doggedness had always carried her through without it. Moreover she had before her the example of her friend's mother, Lady Charlotte Guest, who had translated the Welsh legends and made them a popular, if hardly a scholarly, success. And Lady Charlotte had not waited for the tranquillity of widowhood before undertaking her enormous task. She had accomplished it while running a rich man's establishment, acting as his business secretary, and producing and suckling an almost annual infant.

A few days after her offer, Lady Gregory brought Yeats a specimen of her proposed style, and it appears to have come as a revelation. Thenceforward he was all enthusiasm; more enthusiastic, indeed, than he was ever to be over anything else she did; and this is natural enough, since the two books of translation were the quarry where he was to find material for most of his early plays.

The first book, *Cuchulain of Muirthemne*, took her a year, and at the end of it he wrote to Bridges: 'My friend Lady Gregory has made the most lovely translation, putting the old prose and verse not into the pedantic "hedge school-master" style of her predecessors, but into a musical caressing English, which never goes very far from the idiom of the people she knows so well.'

She did not, of course, translate from the original archaic

Irish, which she made no claim to read. Her 'Dedication to the people of Kiltartan' makes her method plain, as well as getting in a nice dig at Trinity:

'When I went looking for the stories in the old writings, I found that the Irish in them is too hard for any person to read that has not made a long study of it. Some scholars have worked well at them, Irishmen and Germans and Frenchmen, but they have printed them in the old cramped Irish, with translations into German or French or English, and these are not easy for you to get, or to understand, and the stories themselves are confused, every one giving a different account from the others in some small thing, the way there is not much pleasure in reading them. It is what I have tried to do, to take the best of the stories, or whatever parts of each will fit best to one another, and that way to give a fair account of Cuchulain's life and death. I left out a good deal I thought you would not care about for one reason or another, but I put in nothing of my own that could be helped, only a sentence or so now and again to link the different parts together. I have told the whole story in plain and simple words, in the same way my old nurse Mary Sheridan used to be telling stories from the Irish long ago, and I a child at Roxborough.

'And indeed if there was more respect for Irish things among the learned men that live in the college at Dublin, where so many of these old writings are stored, this work would not have been left to a woman of the house, that has to be minding the place, and dividing her share of food.'

Her aim is popularisation, not scholarship; and she returns to the point in her notes to the second book, *Gods and Fighting Men* (1904):

'I believe that those who have once learnt to care for the stories of Cuchulain of Muirthemne, and of Finn and Lugh and Etain, and to recognise the enduring belief in an invisible world and an immortal life behind the visible and the mortal, will not be content with my redaction, but will go, first, to the fuller versions of the best scholars, and then to the manuscripts themselves.'

Yeats contributed a long and enthusiastic preface to *Cuchulain*, which helped greatly to arouse interest in the book, but which also contained the injudicious assertion that her work was definitive, and would make it unnecessary for anyone, 'except now and then for a scientific purpose,' to consult another text. And this exposed her to attack by people who chose to observe only what he had claimed for her, and not what she had claimed for herself.

But if scholars might mutter, as popularisations the two books triumphed, and each of them had gone into four editions by the outbreak of the first world war. They did in fact open the eyes of thousands for the first time to the splendour of their own literary heritage; even an enemy like Maud Gonne admitted that they were 'a real joy to people like myself, who were unable to read the old Irish texts and records'. They took the 'dignity of Ireland' to England and to America; President Theodore Roosevelt was to tell her later how he had made *Cuchulain* his favourite bedside book.

For it was at this time that she found her phrase, 'We work to add dignity to Ireland', one well suited to the work of pious literary patriotism on which she was engaged. As war-cry of the creative movement it was not, I feel, so happy. For literary creation is something that has to be undertaken for its own sake; that it adds dignity to the country of its origin is a mere by-product. To allow an ulterior motive, even a patriotic one, is to open the door to pomposity and rhetoric, and there were people in the movement who took themselves quite seriously enough as it was. Fortunately neither Synge nor Lady Gregory herself was influenced by any notion of 'adding dignity to Ireland' when they came to write their plays.

9

As to the content of the two books, I cannot see that they make Lady Gregory a 'creator', as Yeats claimed. They are no more 'creation' than the *Letter Box* was; that is an honour

reserved for her plays. They are translations, sensitively done
and full of fresh-airy charm, but still the imagery is that of
the anonymous poets. She has not invented it.

How readable she is compared with what has gone before
can be gauged by a glance at her kinsman Standish O'Grady's
Silva Gadelica (1892), which assembles odd incidents with no
attempt to link them into a consecutive story, and translates
them into a style which is an unattractive combination of
pedantry and fancy-dress. Here is his version of a passage
from the Finn saga, the quarrel at Almhuin:

'And then he went over to Goll mac Morna and in front of him
recited the forts, the destructions, the cattle-liftings, the wooings
of his elders and progenitors; by operation of which artistic
efforts the sons of Morna grew jovial and of good cheer.'

And here is the same passage from *Gods and Fighting Men*:

'And then he went over to Goll, son of Morna, and told the
fights and the destructions and the cattle-drivings and the courtings
of his fathers; and it is well-pleased and high-minded the sons of
Morna were, listening to that.'

(O'Grady, incidentally, was no friend to Lady Gregory's
popularisation, despite the kinship, and he disapproved still
more strongly of putting the sagas on to the Abbey stage.
His was the aristocratic view, that a literature which had come
from the people would be vulgarised if it were allowed to go
back to them.)

Not that Lady Gregory's two books are invariably easy
going. There are many scenes of human warmth, and there is
much wild poetry, especially in the songs and laments. But
the ancient heroic outlook is undeniably alien, and among
the lengthy battles and genealogies I suspect that many readers
must have found a tendency to skip. What they fastened on —
and what the poets and dramatists principally took for their
themes — are the two great love-tragedies, the story of

Deirdre which is the crown of the Cuchulain saga, and the story of Grania and her dealings with Diarmuid and with Finn, king and hero of *Gods and Fighting Men*.

One fact may be noted here about these stories, that in each of them the woman makes the running. Deirdre runs literally after Naoise, shrieking so that for very shame he has to turn back. Grania 'puts bonds' on a Diarmuid totally unwilling to leave his honoured and happy place at the court of Finn. The significance of these episodes may have been lost upon some who were to attempt modern interpretations of the ancient mind, but it was not lost upon the translator, as the event was to show.

IV

Renascence II: Apprentice Playwright

I do not propose to re-tell the story of the Abbey Theatre. It has been covered by those whose close connexion with it qualifies them to speak: generally by Dr Lennox Robinson in *Ireland's Abbey Theatre*, and in more detail for the years of the Fays' activities, 1899 to 1908, by Mr Gerard Fay in *The Abbey Theatre, Cradle of Genius*. My concern is primarily with Lady Gregory not as organiser but as writer, and I make no apology for telescoping into the smallest possible space those parts of the Abbey's history that have no direct bearing on her plays.

For three successive years, 1899 to 1901, English companies were brought over to Dublin to present new Irish plays. One may picture Coole humming with excited conferences under the catalpa tree on the lawn, Edward Martyn walking constantly over from Tullira and staying to dine, George Moore finally staying (for the first and last time, for she still could not endure him) in the house. This was when he and Yeats collaborated on a *Diarmuid and Grania* play which was given on the third occasion, and the birth-pangs of which provide Moore with some of *Ave*'s most riotously funny pages. Doubtless the story has not lost in his telling, but it fully explains Lady Gregory's deciding that if Yeats required, as he seemed to do, a dramatic collaborator, then in future it had better be herself.

She had her share in *Diarmuid* too, besides receiving with

apparent meekness Yeats's suggestion that Moore should first write it in French, and she then translate it into her 'speech of the people', which they had not yet begun to call 'Kiltartan'. She says in *Our Irish Theatre* that she began by writing bits of dialogue when wanted; Yeats would dictate to her, and she would suggest a sentence here and there. And so she came to consider the technique of playwriting 'to which I had never given much thought before. I had never cared much for the stage, although when living a good deal in London, my husband and I went, as others do, to see some of each season's plays.'

Douglas Hyde was persuaded that it would help the spread of Irish if the Gaelic League put on vernacular plays, and that he must set to work to write one. They found him a story from Yeats's *Red Hanrahan* folk-series (but he knew it already, for it is quoted in the *Love Songs*), and from it he wrote *The Twisting of the Rope*, a Gaelic lark which may be summarised as 'how to get a troublesome poet out of the house without actually incurring his curse'. It made a much happier impression in Dublin than *Diarmuid*, acted by the F. R. Benson Company, who could not even pronounce the Irish names aright. The Irish playlet was acted by members of the Dublin Gaelic League, with the author in the chief part; a photograph shows him, eyes agleam and walrus moustache rampant, making exuberant love to a lady who looks plain terrified. The producer was a young Dubliner named William Fay.

For Yeats had made an exciting discovery: there were Irish actors after all. They were a company of Dublin amateurs, mainly working-class, who under the direction of Fay and his elder brother Frank were putting on little sketches and farces in coffee-houses and temperance clubs. Their material was poor because they could find no better, but Frank was a man of wide culture, who knew far more about theatrical history than Yeats: he was particularly interested in the modern French methods. Willie had been a professional, and learnt his craft the hard way as a strolling player in 'fit-up' theatres all over Ireland, but he also had an electrician's trade at his finger-tips. They collaborated with Maud Gonne, who had formed a revolutionary women's society called the Daughters of Erin, and helped her to put on patriotic tableaux, and thus they came to the notice of Yeats.

Finding them changed everything. One could begin to write, to think, in genuinely Irish terms. No matter that Martyn had lost interest and withdrawn his financial support. The Fays were 'full of courage', as Lady Gregory records. With incredible doggedness they rented little halls in the back streets of Dublin, did the manual work of conversion themselves, wired and scene-painted, and night after night put their long-suffering amateur actors through those gruelling rehearsals which were to evolve exquisitely clear speaking and a quite new style of acting, simple, unfussy, sincere. It would eventually carry the fame of the Abbey players, and a good many of the players themselves, round the world.

2

Yeats could not put into theatrical terms a dream he had had 'of a cottage where there was well-being and firelight and talk of a marriage, and into the midst of that cottage there came an old woman in a long cloak. She was Ireland herself, that Kathleen ni Houlihan for whom so many songs have been sung and for whose sake so many have gone to their death.' There was a snag, however. 'I could not get down from that high window of dramatic verse, and in spite of all you had done for me, I had not the country speech. One has to live among the people, like you, of whom an old man said in my hearing "She has been a serving-maid among us", before one can think with the thoughts of the people and speak with their tongue. We turned my dream into the little play, *Kathleen ni Houlihan*, and when we gave it to the little theatre in Dublin and found that the working people liked it, you helped me to put my other dramatic fables into speech.'

So Yeats writes in his dedication of the play to Lady Gregory. Short of being actually in the library at Coole with them, one cannot put one's finger on what is his and what is hers. The naturalness and life of the peasant family (even though they do not yet speak with the richness of mature 'Kiltartan') suggest that everything is hers except the symbolic speeches of Kathleen; in a word, that he thought of it and she wrote it; and this is the assertion made to me by the Gregory family, who had many times heard it from her own lips.

Later in his career, Yeats would tend to forget the obligation he had so publicly and honestly acknowledged, and to speak of *Kathleen* as though it were entirely his own. But when her family protested, and urged her to stake her claim, she always refused with a smile, saying that she could not take from him any part of what had proved, after all, his one real popular success.

3

Valuable as the Fays were to all the new dramatists of the movement, they were of particular importance to Lady Gregory. Her plays, based on the folk-mind and the folk-speech, could not have been interpreted without them, and would probably never have been conceived. The talents of Willie Fay as producer and comedian made him her indispensable instrument.

For the moment, however, there was no question of the brothers being anybody's instrument; the initiative had passed to them, and with it the right to choose the plays. Yeats's dramatic society was merged with theirs, and at first Lady Gregory was not even a member, though she subscribed, and urged her friends to subscribe, to its pathetically slender funds.

It was on her way back from the spring visit to Enid Layard in 1902 that her thoughts turned first to a play of her own:

'I did not aspire to a stage production, but I thought a little play in rhyme might perhaps be learned and acted by Kiltartan school-children; and it was on the railway journey home, through Italy and the Alps to Calais, that to the rhythm of the engine I began putting into rhyme the legend of St Colman's birth, as I had heard it from the old people, my neighbours. Monsignor Fahy, then our parish priest, was pleased with it and approved.'

Its simple undenominational piety might well please Dr Fahy, but it would certainly not have passed the Fays. In the verse the engine rhythm is all too evident, and in construction it is the typical amateur's play, all long narrations and happenings 'off'.

All the more astonishing, then, is the advance shown by the second play, which she wrote in the course of the summer, and which was her first acted and her first fully creative work. It is the story of a young man who deliberately loses all his savings on a game of cards, to rescue the husband of his former sweetheart from ruin. She called it by the name of the card-game, which by a convenient coincidence was a number half that of her own years: *Twenty-Five*.

The Fays at first rejected it, on the quaint grounds that to represent a young man as saving a hundred pounds in a two years' stay in America would encourage emigration. But Yeats had already established his ascendancy over them. Presumably he insisted, for the play was put into rehearsal at Christmas, and given in March of the next year. It had a very real success. The critic of the *United Irishman*, perhaps Arthur Griffith himself, found that though the rest of the characteri-sation was slight, Christie, the lover, was a fine character, and said of his final speech, 'It will be long before those who heard it forget it, or forget the play it was spoken in.'

In May it formed part of the repertory on the flying visit to

London which first spread the fame of the new movement overseas, and Yeats reported to her that it went very well and that Willie Fay was charming as Christie. (He had played the elderly husband in the Dublin production.) Wilfrid Scawen Blunt, who was just recovering from influenza, now saw it (together with Yeats's *The Hour-Glass* which he calls 'a terrible infliction'), and noted in his diary: 'It is quite the most perfect little work of art and the most touching play I have ever seen acted. Only it made me weep in my weak state.' It is true that Blunt was a close friend, but that did not lessen his critical faculties. Later on he found another play of hers, *The Image*, tedious, and did not scruple to say so.

Only one person decided, on reflection, that she could not bear *Twenty-Five*, and that was the author. 'Weak', 'sentimental', 'a storehouse of the faults of my dramatic method'; again and again she castigates her unfortunate first-born. She would not have it included in the first collection of her one-act plays, the *Seven Short Plays* of 1909. As far as was possible to her, she blotted it out.

Fortunately it was not possible. *The Gael*, the monthly magazine of the American Gaelic League, was in the habit of printing in advance texts of the Irish dramatic movement which was proving of so much interest to Irish-American sympathisers, and in its issue for December 1902 I found the text of *Twenty-Five*, under the title of *A Losing Game*, and am therefore able to add my voice to Blunt's. If Willie Fay could come back from the dead to act it for me, I feel certain he would have no difficulty in reducing me also to tears.

4

To start with, I do not find it badly constructed. True, Christie returns from America rather pat after he has been talked of, but that is dramatic licence. His interview with Kate is touching, and may well have echoes of those exiles' letters written and answered at Roxborough. Why could she not have waited for him? — he cries. Because her parents had died in the meantime, she was afraid of being a burden, and because he never wrote, she answers, and he tells her: 'If I didn't write oftener, I was never a great hand at writing, and the thoughts I had of you were enough to go round the world of themselves.'

But what's done is done; they are fine young people, and there is no thought of her running away from her decent elderly husband. All the assurance Christie asks is that she is happy and prosperous. But she is not; Michael has had bad luck and must sell up, and they must go wandering to Manchester, that remote and dreadful place, where he has a cousin; 'the poor have all the trouble of the world.'

Christie draws out his savings, a hundred pounds. 'I got it all changed into sovereigns and notes, the way we could be looking at it and counting it together.' He had landed in America with one sovereign, and that he had never spent, but kept it to buy her wedding-ring. She repulses his offer. Michael could never accept it, and nor could she.

Michael returns with some neighbours for a farewell drink; Christie introduces himself as a chance traveller who has come 'looking for treasure', and is hospitably included. He proposes the card-game, which to Yeats was the weak element in the play. And admittedly it is tricky to put on the stage any sort of game in which the audience cannot share, but Lady Gregory has, I consider, overcome this very skilfully by focussing attention on Kate and her increasingly hysterical attempts to get the game stopped and tell Michael the truth. There is a cunning use of phrases that mean one thing to Kate and the audience, another to Michael and his friends. 'Take back your money, Christie,' she cries, and he answers: 'There are some things no man can take back, and they once gone from him.'

And so he loses his hundred pounds, 'all but five', and assures them that it's nothing, he has plenty more where that comes from, and one of them says wistfully: 'It must be a grand thing to be rich.'

'It's a grand thing indeed,' says Christie. 'It's a grand thing to be free in the world, and not to be tied to your little bit of ground, in dread of the drought in the spring-time and the rain in the harvest. It's a grand thing not to be shut up in a little narrow house, keeping a watch on the little store you have hid under the hearth-stone, and the wife you have maybe begrudging you the use of it in your lifetime. It's a grand thing to be able to take up your money in your hand, and to think no more of it when it slips away than you would of a trout that would slip back into the stream!'

Then the fiddler strikes up, and he demands a dance from Kate; she is sobbing and refuses him, but he insists. 'Give me a dance now, and I'll be thinking of you sometimes when I'm dancing with some high-up lady having golden shoes, in a marble court by the sea.' He takes his costly kiss, and goes out of her life.

Why did Lady Gregory 'take against' *Twenty-Five*? Most of the faults she charges it with seem to me baseless, but in her charge that it is sentimental, I think we have the answer. From the first it was vital to her to write honestly, from her direct experience, putting down what she knew about the people, not what she would have liked to believe. In their different ways all of the movement aimed at this honesty; lack of it was, in their opinion, what had brought the fashionable London theatre into vulgarity and disrepute. And to Lady Gregory it must have seemed utterly unlikely, thinking the matter over, that any Irish peasant like Christie (or, if we believe that already with her the peasant stands for all Irishmen, then any Irishman at all) would have given up his fortune for a fruitless love. For love of home or country, yes; for love of a woman, no. Romantic love was not a ruling passion, she had noted of the Aran Islanders. Nothing she had observed of the rest of her countrymen could conscientiously permit her to modify this view.

And so the wistful little *Twenty-Five*, that brings a lump into the sentimental English throat, was judged and condemned. It was not, however, so soon exorcised. The idea of the benevolent deception was used again in *The Jackdaw*, and finally in old age she rewrote the actual play, calling it *On the Racecourse*, and effectively banishing sentiment by making all three protagonists worthless. The husband becomes a callous wastrel, the wife a sulky slut and the lover a ninny. And then there seems no point to the story any more.

V

Comedy

The decade from 1902 to 1912, when she was between fifty and sixty, was the most productive period of Lady Gregory's career, and in it she wrote all but two of the plays by which, in my opinion, she is likely to be remembered. It was also the Abbey's greatest period, which saw the flowering of Synge's genius and the efforts of his ungrateful countrymen to get it suppressed; and she took rather more than her share in the long struggle to get the theatre established on a sound financial basis, to find it new playwrights, and to secure for them all, but for Synge especially, complete freedom of speech.

I hope I have shown that her life up till now had been intellectually active, and scotched the myth of the simple country lady waiting in rural domesticity at Coole for Yeats to wave his magic wand. Even so, this sudden outburst of intense creative activity has in it something miraculous, something of a genuine 'rebirth'. So has Synge's, but one feels in him the febrile energy of a man whose time is short. With Lady Gregory, it is sheer joyous exuberance at the discovery of her right road. She takes the bit between her teeth, and away she runs.

The days of the little makeshift playhouses were ending. Synge's two first plays, *In the Shadow of the Glen* and *Riders to the Sea*, had been read aloud by her at a literary party in Queen Anne's Mansions in January of 1903; the first of them was put on at the Molesworth Hall in October, and the second in February of the next year. But by then it was known that Yeats's friend Miss Horniman, a minor heiress of the Manchester tea firm, was going to give them a theatre, a small and modest affair, but technically equipped with all that was needed, and princely compared with what they had been enduring. The old Mechanics' Institute in Abbey Street, only a step from Sackville Street and from the Liffey, was bought and converted, (part of it had also at one time been the City Morgue, and there were pleasing stories of corpses mislaid).

Conversion took longer than had been expected, and there was also trouble over securing a patent. When secured, it had to be vested in someone resident in the country, which Miss Horniman was not, and it was granted to 'Dame Augusta Gregory', who had to promise, among other things, not to allow women and children to be hung from the flies or to exhibit wild beasts on the stage. The title was a pure formality, of course, but it helped to strengthen Lady Gregory's position — and to weaken Miss Horniman's.

The Abbey Theatre opened on December 27th, 1904, and it was also the first night of Lady Gregory's first comedy, *Spreading the News*. She herself was ill at Coole and could not be there, but Miss Horniman was among the ladies present, according to the account in the *Irish Times*. One surmises that Lady Gregory's absence was not much regretted by Miss Horniman, who could feel for the first and last time that the theatre was really her own.

For it quickly became known in Dublin that Lady Gregory and the new benefactress did not hit it off, and if not all the speculation was on the lines of that I have quoted from Maud Gonne, a version which was, and still is, more generally believed shows Lady Gregory as the aristocrat making use of Miss Horniman's money, but despising her because she was middle-class and her money came from trade.

This accusation of snobbery is a stick commonly used to

beat Lady Gregory with, by those who had reason to think
she did not like them. 'Peer or peasant — she had no use for
anyone in between,' I have been told. But bourgeois
Philistinism has never endeared itself to any writer of talent,
and as displayed by the Irish middle classes of her day, it was
slightly more colourful than its English equivalent, but
intrinsically just as boring. Far too many people made racing,
gambling and gossip the principal objects of their lives, and
in consequence she could have nothing in common with
them. Nor, for that matter, could Yeats or Synge, but her
disapproval was more resented than theirs, because she was a
woman and graciousness was expected of her.

In an intensely class-conscious age, she judged people, it
seems to me, principally for what they were. It is not always
easy to acquit her of intellectual snobbery, but of simple
social snobbery she was remarkably free. If the first generation
of Abbey actors were not treated as equals by the three
playwriting Directors, it was because they were not equals;
they were not people of any education, except for the self-
taught Frank Fay, and Yeats himself contrasts Maire nic
Shiubhlaigh, the leading lady, with 'women of our class'.
When by personality or talent any of them outgrew this
handicap, the treatment altered; Sara Allgood, for example,
became an intimate friend of Lady Gregory and a frequent
visitor to Coole. And if Lady Gregory had misgivings over
Synge's engagement to Maire O'Neill, so had Sara Allgood,
who was Maire's own sister; in view of the disparity in age,
education and temperament, one may share their doubts that
the marriage would have been a happy one.

To Lady Gregory, social snobbery is always material for
satire, or if it occurs among her near and dear, for concern.
When Hugh Lane, who was later to become her favourite
among her nephews, first started as a picture-dealer in London,
he antagonised her by 'hankering, as I thought, after coronets

and fashion'. She was careless of her position in Galway county society, and her carelessness gave offence, traces of which linger still. It is remembered that the door of Coole was always open to Kiltartan villagers and Gort townsfolk, but that county ladies, arriving in their carriages to pay a social call, would as likely as not be told that her Ladyship was not at home. I am reliably informed that after Sir William's death she dropped his relations, which was no doubt reprehensible. But the attitude of the county as a whole can be summed up in the remark made by 'some old ladies, our neighbours,' about Hyde's first visit: 'He cannot be a gentleman if he speaks Irish.' It was the attitude she had resented all through her youth at Roxborough, and if she showed snobbery now, it was snobbery in reverse.

What she loved best was talent; and what exasperated her was the burying of talent by those who 'let their lives run to waste'. And she was ready to encourage all talents, not merely her own literary kind; her benevolence in the circle of nieces proves that. None of them were writers, but two were musically gifted, a third wished to become a painter, a fourth a professional gardener (something quite out of the way for a young lady at that date); and it was always Aunt Augusta who interceded with their parents to let them leave home and be properly trained.

As for the suggestion that she despised money made from trade, it is on the face of it ludicrous. She would have had to despise the Guinness money, which on many occasions saved the Abbey and was always received by her with unfeigned gratitude. (And for that matter, Roxborough itself had once possessed a distillery, the chimney of which remains.) Financial fastidiousness at the Abbey was the prerogative of the idealists, who often enough made Lady Gregory's rich friends a reproach to her, but were glad all the same to get their fingers on what she could beg.

To return to Miss Horniman: it appears to me that Lady Gregory made a genuine effort to like her, invited her to Coole (an honour not conferred on any of Yeats's other women intimates) and welcomed her as a friend. And indeed, she had much in her which would command Lady Gregory's respect. She was honest, single-minded in her devotion to the theatre, and a tremendous worker. Her fortune at this time was not large, so that by spending most of it on the Abbey she obliged herself to live simply; and she was quite touchingly happy to be included in its creative work, and allowed to design costumes, which she also stitched. Unfortunately, her designing talent was meagre.

If Lady Gregory failed to like Miss Horniman, it was partly for the reason why a good many other people in Ireland failed to like her, that by Irish standards she was not an ingratiating person. Even by English standards she was out-spoken to a degree; and in Ireland, where it is customary to wrap up disagreement or rebuke in soft words, she must have seemed brutally rude almost every time she opened her mouth, or put pen to yellow paper in those acrimonious letters that made Synge say he ever afterwards hated the colour of daffodils.

There was also, more importantly, a cleavage of intention between them, which was widened as time went on. Miss Horniman may or may not have been in love with Yeats, but she was certainly in love with his genius, which she believed to be that of a playwright. In him she saw a second Shakespeare, and her theatre was to be his Globe. She cared nothing for 'adding dignity to Ireland', or for any other Irish playwrights or aspirations, which were lumped by her together as 'hole-and-corner Irish ideas'.

Lady Gregory cared first and foremost for the poetic plays of Yeats; we know this because she says so, in the vital 'Play-writing' chapter of *Our Irish Theatre*. But if they were

'the apex of the flame, the point of the diamond', they were
not with her the only reason for the theatre's existence. There
were also Ireland's dignity, and the discovery and encouragement of new authors, and lastly there was her own creative
talent and its need for an outlet. Because she invariably speaks
of it modestly, because she too often adopts (in my opinion
mistakenly) a deprecatory tone, we should not therefore
underestimate it as a driving force within her. All talent
drives its possessor, and comes in the end to matter more than
the genius, be it never so lofty, of a friend.

Miss Horniman's whole attitude to the Abbey, to Lady
Gregory, and to the Fays, which their family historian finds
so baffling, can be explained, it seems to me, in the light of
her increasing disappointment as the poetic plays of Yeats
failed to score more than a *succès d'estime*. That Lady Gregory's
own plays were meanwhile having a real, popular, side-
splitting and tear-jerking success only turned the knife in the
wound. But if Lady Gregory had never written a line, she
would still have got on to 'Miss Horniman's list of truly
wicked people', because she stood for Ireland. And that was
not what the tea-merchant's granddaughter had ordered when
she invested her twenty thousand pounds in an 'artistic'
theatre of which the major achievement was to be the poetic
drama of Yeats.

2

The double bill of the opening night was Yeats's Cuchulain
play *On Baile's Strand*, which contains some of his most
beautiful dramatic verse, and *Spreading the News*. One of his
curious dramatic theories was that the proper emotion to be
induced by tragedy should be 'an ever-deepening reverie',
which sounds suspiciously like saying that the audience dozed
off. If they did, then *Spreading the News* woke them up with a
bang.

'We got a tremendous pace into it,' says Willie Fay in his autobiography, 'the pace of a hard football match.' When, later on, it was taken to England, the pace had to be modified. English audiences, less quick-witted than Dublin and with ears not attuned to Irish speech, simply could not take it in.

Flowering as it did so late in her life, the working of her talent always fascinated Lady Gregory, and when she came to print her plays, she included a note on the origins of each, which is of inestimable benefit to her literary biographer. *Spreading the News* was, it seems, intended to be another wistful piece like *Twenty-Five*; the Russian-scandal theme was to be used to rob a girl at a fair of her good name. But Yeats felt that something more amusing was needed to offset the poetic plays which made up most of the theatre's tiny repertory. Having grown interested in the girl, she found difficulty in inventing another central character with some depth to him, till she hit on the idea of Bartley, the henpecked little man who takes a lugubrious joy in his own misfortunes, and gets his supreme reward by being cast for the part of the assassin as the myth, with a bubbling wealth of comic invention, monstrously grows.

For sheer high spirits perhaps it stands at the top of her list. It is still acted, though at the Abbey more often in Irish than in English. It was translated, pirated, even made (quite unsuitably, one would think) into a comic opera. Nobody could deny its success with the audience, but those whose heads were still in the Celtic twilight spoke of it sneeringly as a pleasing little anecdote, a mere farce. It is true that she was to do better technically, but the thing is the work of a mature dramatic personality, showing us in miniature the kind of playwright she is, and how she differs from her great contemporaries, Yeats and Synge.

They differ widely from each other, but each in his way is

a romantic; she is classic. She has gone for her lessons, not to Maeterlinck or to the minor Elizabethans, but to Molière and Congreve. (The plays of Congreve was one of the six books she would have taken in that library legacy at Coole.) She who had been living for the last three years in the cloudy world of the ancient epics shows no trace of their influence when she comes to choose the form in which she will express herself. It is neat, taut, finished; a conundrum has been set and successfully solved. The classic approach was not fashionable in 1904, and neatness was bound to seem anecdotal. What matters, however, is not the form in which you express yourself, but the quality of what you have to express.

And the little play is not a mere farce, firstly because Bartley is a real human being, even if the scandal-mongers weaving their web round him are two-dimensional, and secondly because its underlying intention is serious. She is laughing at her characters, as every writer of comedy does, but she is laughing at what is universal in them, not at what is accidental or ephemeral; certainly not at what is 'peasant'. She is not even merely satirising 'the incorrigible Irish genius for myth-making'; the Irish may bring an extra bravura to the art, but we all practise it. We all relish a scandal, and take care to pass it on in better shape than we receive it. The credulous market-folk of *Spreading the News* have their counterparts in the drawing-room.

And so it was to be in all her comedies. *Hyacinth Halvey* was inspired by 'a well-dressed, well-brushed man' in the Abbey stalls. The counterparts of the paupers of *The Workhouse Ward*, kept alive by their joy in a quarrel, could be found in a St James's clubroom. And her cleverest technical feat, *The Bogie Men*, in which the protagonists are two chimney-sweeps, was the favourite with the elegant and worldly Hugh Lane, because, he said, it exactly paralleled his experience with his cousins.

3

Hyacinth Halvey was written about the same time as she made the first of her direct translations of Molière into 'Kiltartan', and it has strong echoes of Molière, being almost entirely a series of ding-dong duets. One of them develops into that typical Molière device, the dialogue that is really two separate monologues, neither party really listening to the other. Willie Fay, who as her first producer is always illuminating about her work, liked this the best of her short comedies, and I daresay he is right. The contrast is in itself piquant between the elegance of the rhythm and the artlessness of what the characters actually say.

As characters, they have more to them than those of *Spreading the News*; they are fewer in number and the play is a little longer. (In future her tendency will be to pare the numbers in her casts.) The theme of 'give a dog a good name and refuse to hang him' is carried through with the greatest gusto and fertility of invention. Hyacinth the new Sub-Sanitary Inspector, burdened with his dewy innocence and his wonderful testimonials, including one from the Resident Magistrate ('it is very kind of him indeed, and he not knowing me at all'), is nicely set off by the bustling interference of the postmistress and the priest's housekeeper, the ruthless stage-management of the police-sergeant, and the sneaking sympathy of the unregenerate telegraph boy. And then there is Mr Quirke the butcher, one of Nature's publicity-agents, beneath whose praises the strongest would quail.

Lady Gregory's characters are commonly lumped under the heading 'peasant', but in fact many of them are peasant only in the sense of not being Ascendancy; they have a much wider social range than the characters of Synge. Here, Hyacinth the small official, the postmistress and the housekeeper would be greatly affronted at being taken for tillers of the soil, and the managing sergeant is a Protestant, although graciously prepared to accept the priest's support on the platform; 'No bigotry about me when there is a question of the welfare of any fellow-creatures.'

They are all townsfolk, and we are in the Square at Gort, imperfectly concealed under the name of Cloon. That Mr Quirke had his original there we know from the *Journals*, and I am told there was a postmistress who really did read the postcards (and mysteriously divined the contents of letters too). And in the next play, *The Jackdaw*, Mrs Broderick speaks of being 'better pleased going to my burying at the Seven Churches'; the unique and exquisite ruins at Kilmacduagh are in use as the town's burying-ground, in a manner somewhat disconcerting to the English antiquarian mind. The two hotels mentioned, Noonan's Royal and Mack's, flourish still as Lally's Royal and Glynn's.

(It is not surprising that as the fame of their new playwright spread back to Gort, some of her originals should have taken umbrage, and that one of them was heard to declare that her Ladyship should get a good slap in a particular quarter. What they could hardly be expected to appreciate was the extent to which she had lifted their characters from the particular to the universal.)

For myself, I find *The Jackdaw* even better fun, because of the superb character of Joseph Nestor, a wiseacre worthy to stand beside Dogberry with his two gowns and his losses. 'One Joseph Nestor I am, there are few in the district but know me. Indeed they all have a great opinion of me. Travelled I did in the army, and attended school and I young, and slept in the one bed with two boys that were learning Greek.'

Joseph keeps himself up to date with *Tit-Bits* and *Home Chat*, and when Mrs Broderick's skinflint brother wants to help her out of her financial difficulties, without revealing his identity for fear of being put upon (here is the benevolent

deception of *Twenty-Five* with the sentiment taken out of it),
it is Joseph who thinks up a plan. She shall be paid ten pounds
for her jackdaw, and told that it comes from a South African
millionaire who fancies a jackdaw to keep him company
down in his mine. Whereupon the whole town starts collecting jackdaws, the skinflint brother as keenly as any. 'It seems
to me to have set fire to a rick,' observes Joseph, adding
confidently: 'but I am well able to quench it after.' He has,
however, underestimated his countrymen's talent for wishful-
thinking, and we leave him about to be consumed in his own
flames.

As, presumably, he was, for he does not reappear in the
cast of *The Full Moon* (1910), which tells what happened
afterwards to Hyacinth, Mrs Broderick and Bartley, and like
most sequels is on the whole a mistake.

The two of her comedies which have had the widest
success are *The Rising of the Moon* and *The Workhouse Ward*,
but as these are, partly by reason of that same success, the two
that have been most persistently attributed to Yeats and to
Hyde respectively, I will leave discussion of them until I come
to consider the whole subject of her 'collaborators', and what,
if anything, they gave her. Both plays were put on, like *The
Jackdaw*, in 1907, which date also saw her noble one-act folk
tragedy *Dervorgilla*, and her involvement in the *Playboy* row,
and may perhaps be held her year of greatest all-round
achievement.

The last two short comedies have only two characters each.
To pull off this sort of sleight-of-hand requires immense
technical skill, and she manages it unfalteringly. In *Coats*, the
editors of rival weeklies in the provincial town (we have
moved to Galway, and I hope the editors of the *Connacht
Tribune* and the *Galway Observer* are listening) dine together
and exchange coats by mistake. Each then draws out of a
pocket an obituary of himself written by the other. She has

Lady Gregory in 1903, by J. B. Yeats the Elder. Reproduced by courtesy of the National Gallery of Ireland.

put her finger unerringly on the things we take offence at, which are seldom if ever the things we need to be ashamed of; and she shows a right understanding of the journalist's mind in their final decision not to destroy the offending pieces, because 'there is nothing ails them only to begin a good way after the start, and to stop before the finish', and instead to 'put such part of them as we do not need at this time back on the shelf of the press'.

The idea of *The Bogie Men* came to her during the Abbey company's first American tour, being based, she says, on a story of his childhood told to her by her Philadelphian host, and like the rest of her comic fables it is universal in its application, but it is also 'our incorrigible genius for myth-making' carried to the extreme of the creature terrified by its own myth. To say more of it would be to give its game away; I can only salute a miraculous little *tour de force*.

4

There remain the two longer comedies, *Damer's Gold*, which has two acts, and *The Image*, which has the full three. She herself called *The Image* 'my chief play', it was the only one she insisted on having revived, and Dr Lennox Robinson likewise 'gives it the branch'. Yeats on the other hand said it was too slow in action and had an act too many, and reluctantly I find myself in agreement with him; indeed, I would say it has two acts too many. The notion of the statue to be erected to a non-existent hero, with the prob-lematic profits to be made from the oil of two evanescent whales, would have done nicely for a second *Jackdaw*, which was what she originally intended.

But then it became involved with her theory of the 'heart-secret', the cherished dream that keeps each one of us alive, and ought never to have its impracticability revealed by being told aloud. To carry the weight of this symbolic meaning, she

G

expanded the little story, and as so often happens, the meaning has escaped her and gone into a programme-note instead of into the play itself. Its only explicit statement is in the last-act speech of old Peggy, who is not a sufficiently impressive character to pervade, as she needs to do, the whole play. To say that is not to deny that the actual workmanship of *The Image*, the dialogue, the characters of the pushing wife and the three elderly men with their alternate vauntings and self-doubtings, are among her very best.

She translated *L'Avare* in 1908, and Damer of *Damer's Gold* (1912) is a worthy younger brother to the great Harpagon; no mere copy, but an Irish miser, bringing to his hoarding an extra quality of Celtic imagination. He longs to have his jar of gold so full that when he shakes it there will be no rattle. 'Weightier it gets and weightier, but there will always be that little sound. I thought to stop it one time, putting in a fistful of hayseed; but I felt in my heart that was not dealing fair and honest with myself, and I rose up and shook it out again, rising up in my bed in the night time.' In a scene of true Molièresque quality he proceeds to try and wheedle out of his pauper nephew the gold piece which is the latter's sole fortune. 'You wouldn't think now how quiet I would sleep, and the good dreams that would be going through me, and that gallon jar to be full and to make no sound the time I would roll it on the floor. That would be a great deed for one little pound piece to do!'

He has exactly the right relatives. There are Delia his sister, loud in her protests of disinterestedness, and her yes-man husband:

Delia: I have the first covetous person yet to meet I would like! I never would go thrusting after gold, I to get all Lord Clanricarde's estate.

Ralph: She never would, only at a time she might have her own means spent and consumed.

And there is Simon, the feckless nephew with the one gold piece. He taunts Damer into playing him for it, and wins the whole fortune in a night. Then comes Lady Gregory's subtlest observation on the matter of money, that it carries its own taint with it, that the miser's gold will make fresh misers as it passes on. The reformed Damer is all for a spending spree, but Simon now bethinks him that 'it might be a nice thing for the two of us to start gathering the full of it again'. In her notes to the play, their creator expresses the hope that they arrived at a middle course, but I should back Simon's new-found caution every time.

Dr Lennox Robinson says of this play that it was originally too long, and that during rehearsal he persuaded her to shorten some of her sail. Perhaps the two-act length at which it now stands is awkward for the present-day stage, but it is exactly right for the theme, and the piece combined with, say, *The Jackdaw* would give an evening of high comedy, civilised and sane.

VI

Folk-History

I

It is characteristic of Lady Gregory that having achieved a comic triumph with *Spreading the News*, she did not at once follow it up but turned to something fresh, letting a year elapse before *Hyacinth*. Folk-history, which was in a sense her own discovery, seemed to her eminently suited to the stage, full as it was of dramatic colour and symbolism, and spoken with the people's voice. In *Our Irish Theatre* she half apologetically explains her change of direction.

'Perhaps I ought to have written nothing but these short comedies, but desire for experiment is like fire in the blood, and I had had from the beginning a vision of historical plays being sent by us through all the counties of Ireland. . . . I still hope to see a little season given up every year to plays on history and in sequence at the Abbey, and I think schools and colleges may ask to have them sent and played in their halls, as part of the day's lesson. I began with the daring and lightheartedness of a schoolboy to write a tragedy in three acts upon a great personality, Brian the High King. I made many bad beginnings, and if I had listened to Mr Yeats's advice I should have given it up, but I began again and again till it was at last moulded into at least a possible shape.'

In fact, she must have started thinking about it soon after she finished *Twenty-Five*. Yeats was lecturing in America during the winter of 1903–4, and wrote to know how it was getting on; it was when he came home that he advised her to give it up. I think this is the one complaint against him that she lets slip into print, for she was invariably loyal to him.

But his discouragement over *Kincora* rankled deeply. She was making her first major effort, at a three-act play and one of a quite new kind, and this was the moment when she needed from her friends the sort of sympathy she gave them. She persisted, with her usual doggedness, and a year later he was reporting to Quinn that the play was greatly ennobled and improved. But her recalling the incident to Sean O'Casey, twenty years later, shows that this wound was never quite healed.

Once again she is her own most acute critic, for of the first *Kincora* she says: 'I had not enough of skill to wrestle with the mass of material, and I think I kept too closely to history.' It is certainly a complicated subject. Brian was the Irish Alfred, who welded the country into a unit and drove out the Danes at the cost of his own life. His Achilles' heel was his queen, Gormleith, who had formerly been married to his rival, Malachi, and before that to a leader of the Danes. Explaining these relationships takes up too much of a novice dramatist's time, and she has not helped herself by a supernatural prologue, in which Brian as a youth has his fate prophesied to him by a woman of the Sidhe.

But with all its faults, the first *Kincora* was a success at the Abbey, and its novelty was recognised. Here was half-legendary history treated not in a remote or cloudy way, but vividly and topically, its characters speaking in accents not very different from those of the Galway comedies. The need to drive out the foreigner, the impossibility of doing so while counsels remained divided and leaders were selfish and touchy, were lessons which the year 1014 could teach directly to the year 1905.

Inevitably, Gormleith ran away with the play, and there was a surprising welcome accorded to this Irish Lady Macbeth, this 'torch of baleful womanhood' as one reviewer called her — surprising in view of the cold shoulder turned on poor Nora in Synge's *Shadow of the Glen*. But then Nora's sin was of sex, whereas Gormleith's was only of ambition, though it brought thousands to their deaths. The part was played by Maire nic Shiubhlaigh, the Abbey's first leading lady, an intense and politically-minded young woman who got out of it all that it was worth. The highlight was a quite remarkable trial scene, where Gormleith, under guise of pleading for her life, was in fact making love to Brian, her judge, and emerged triumphantly a free woman and his future queen.

But if critics were kind, the author was still aware that the play was amateurish, and she continued to brood and work over it. The second version, produced in 1909, is an altogether more professional job, tightened, and opening with Brian and Gormleith wedded, which means the sacrifice of the trial scene. But the action has gained greatly in swiftness, and the queen's character in depth and dignity. She is still 'the crow of battle', bored with her queenship in Brian's welfare state, but she is no longer a frivolous mischief-maker, ready to stir up trouble among servants when kings are not to hand. Her treachery is clearly and even sympathetically motivated. She is torn between love for Brian and love for her Danish son, she is politically clear-sighted and gives her husband wise advice, and what is her reward? With half his thoughts on heaven, he turns from her to the counsels of a saintly beggar-woman, he bids her go and pray. Of course she throws in her lot with the Danes, as any creature of spirit would.

She is a most interesting figure, this Gormleith, the first of Lady Gregory's studies of frustrated womanhood. To the end she is splendid; there is something heroic in her farewell to the doomed Brian: 'It is not Brian would wish to die the death of a man that is lessening and stiffening, the time he grows attentive to his bed, but of a winner that is merry and shouting, the time his enemies are put down. I was maybe a right wife for him. A right wife, a lucky wife, in spite of all!'

Would the second *Kincora* revive? It is still a fairly cumbersome subject, requiring close attention from the audience during the first scene, when relationships and motives are being set out; but then, so do most of the historical plays of Shakespeare. It has vitality and a fine heroic swing, and the experiment deserves to be tried.

2

A great source of happiness over *Kincora*, and from then on to *The Image*, was collaboration between mother and son. For Robert Gregory had discovered that his real talent was that of a painter, and had gone on from Oxford to the Slade. Yeats's ideas of stage decoration were much in advance of his time, and he found the ideal interpreter in Robert Gregory, who worked on the early Abbey heroic plays while still a student. His 'Wood of Clontarf' scene for the last act of the first *Kincora* created a sensation, for instead of the conventional stage woodland with every leaf stippled in, it was a pattern of boles of trees with a leaf design applied in one colour, giving a rhythmic grey-green effect. All was done on the usual shoestring budget, Robert painting most of the scenery himself, and dyeing the material for costumes in a great iron pot which was also a useful property in cottage interiors.

Of course the settings for the comedies did not need elaborate staging; she herself saw to it that furniture was authentic by bringing up spinning-wheels and the like from Coole, and many of the peasant costumes were the real thing, bought from an old-clothes shop in Galway and carefully disinfected. But the historical and poetic plays demanded visual beauty, and one who never missed an Abbey first-night of the great decade has recorded his opinion that Robert Gregory's settings were the only ones that achieved real distinction.

Shortage of money alone cannot explain this relative poverty of design, and it is the more to be regretted because the Irish Renascence has its fine-art as well as its literary side. If Edward Martyn had not seceded from the Abbey group, he might most valuably have linked the two.

In any history of the Abbey, Martyn is bound to seem a rather futile figure, but in fact his fine artistic and musical taste enabled him to use his money in ways of which the effects are still being felt. In 1897, the year when the first theatre project began, the foundation-stone was also laid for a new Roman Catholic cathedral in Lady Gregory's home town of Loughrea, and this astonishing building is in its way just as much an achievement of the new creative impulse as are the plays of the Abbey dramatists. Credit for the beauty of everything in it, carving, metalwork, vestments, embroideries, above all stained glass, goes primarily to a series of enlightened Bishops of Clonfert, but Martyn was friend and adviser to the first two, and introduced the artists, Protestant equally with Catholic, who laboured here for the glory of God.

Many of the same names occur at the Abbey and at Loughrea. A Yeats, the poet's painter brother Jack, designed the vestments, together with his wife and Pamela Coleman Smith, and they were embroidered by Lily Yeats and her workgirls of the Cuala Industries. Sarah Purser, who painted many of the Abbey portraits and did the stained glass for the vestibule, founded her 'Tower of Glass' workshop at Martyn's suggestion, primarily to work on the windows for the new cathedral, and thus gave their opportunity to a series of Irish artists, the best-known among them Michael Healy and Evie Hone, who brought back to stained-glass painting the glory it had lost since mediaeval times.

To stand in Loughrea Cathedral of a summer evening, when the western sun filters through Healy's tremendous 'Day of Judgment' window, and through Evie Hone's strong and sensitive 'St Brigid', is to experience almost the same emotion that one would feel at a perfect performance of Synge's *Deirdre* or O'Casey's *Plough and the Stars*. Dignity has indeed been brought back to Ireland; faith is restored in the genius of the race. And one may, perhaps, spare a thought for poor frustrated Edward Martyn, who made so little mark with his own talents, but helped others to make so great a mark with theirs.

3

Before the production of the next folk-history play, *The White Cockade*, in December of 1905, a change had taken place in the constitution of the Abbey which was momentous both for its future and for Lady Gregory's position in it. Hitherto no one had been paid except Willie Fay, who received a very small salary as manager. Now it was felt that the chief actors should be enabled to become professionals and devote their whole time to the work, and Miss Horniman offered to guarantee salaries. The society was put on to a business footing and became a limited liability company, with Yeats, Synge and Lady Gregory as directors. Materially the Fays were thus better off, as they fully deserved to be, but their power had gone. They had become paid employees of what had been largely their own creation and concern.

One can sympathise with Mr Gerard Fay's feeling that this was a mistake, and that one of the Fays ought to have been on the board, and as a matter of common justice this might well have been done. As a matter of theatrical policy, I am not so sure.

The directors were unpaid, and could afford to be. Lady Gregory and Synge had small private incomes, and Yeats the possibility of earning by his pen outside his Abbey work. (So for that matter had Lady Gregory; the steady sale of the two books of translation must have brought in a welcome annual sum till the beginning of the first world war.) It therefore looks like economic discrimination, but it was not. They were the directors because they were the principal playwrights, and if the Fays had achieved, unaided, an actors' theatre, the aim of Yeats and Lady Gregory from the start had been a playwrights' theatre, to combat the abuses of the actor-dominated fashionable stage. They were fiercely determined against any sort of dictation by actors, any 'starring', and I think they were right.

We all have our bias, of course, and mine is naturally towards writers. All art may be, as Synge said, collaboration, but all art is certainly not initiation. The writer alone initiates, the rest interpret and embellish. The greatness of the Abbey, I firmly believe, is due to its having been controlled by the people who initiated. They made their errors and muddles, which is not surprising seeing that they were pioneers and had to evolve their technique as they went along. But they were always on the initiator's side. Their criterion was always: Is this in our judgment a good play? — not, Will this be popular, shall we make money, will it give So-and-So a good part?

And this approach enabled them to discover and promote the work of other dramatists. Actors, one might argue, could equally well have done it, but the fact remains that they did not. Swarm after swarm of actors hived off from a theatre with whose discipline and small pay they were bound to grow discontented as soon as they had achieved fame, and not one of the companies so formed was ever capable of writing any body of plays for itself, or of getting any talent of real importance to write for it. Only the dramatists' theatre proved able to do that.

As long as all within the society were equal, all had a voice in the choice of plays, but the responsibility for reading plays seems early to have passed to Yeats and Lady Gregory, and a formidable burden it was to shoulder in addition to their own writing. Most of the manuscripts were hand-written, and often in poor ink on worse paper, and Yeats declared himself biassed in favour of these, because from among them might be expected that great dramatist of the people whom they all sought.

Occasionally Lady Gregory jibbed; in a letter to Frank Fay she rather pathetically suggests that 'anyone who wants a criticism should be asked to write, with the play, a synopsis of the plot and the idea he is trying to express'. But she never forgot that this toil was an Abbey director's most vital function, and after each Dublin visit would return loaded with scripts to Coole. After some years a committee was formed to weed out the evident rubbish, but anything showing the slightest promise still went to the directors, and often came back from them with suggestions for its improvement, or for the future course the writer might take; it was just such encouragement from Lady Gregory that set O'Casey on his right road.

A further consequence of the policy of keeping the actor down was keeping the producer down too. (In their writings he is usually referred to as stage-manager, but Willie Fay was what we should call a producer today.) This was to be a fruitful source of future trouble, for producers naturally resented having members of the company go to the directors over their heads. But that was the theatre's constitution, and Miss Maureen Delany has confirmed to me that 'Yeats and Lady Gregory would always see you in their rooms and listen to complaints'. And the answer again is, it worked.

The directors, by and large, did the right thing, whereas sundry producers, particularly in the difficult years during and after the first war, did the wrong thing. They grumbled at interference, especially Lady Gregory's, but as a director it was her business to interfere. A happy solution was eventually found in the long reign of a producer who was also dramatist and finally director, Lennox Robinson. But even to him she would not delegate her share of the responsibility, and he has fully and generously acknowledged that she was right.

An aristocracy of talent ruled the Abbey henceforward; there remains the lingering suspicion that it was also an aristocracy of blood. I do not think it is justified. Why the creative talent in those first years should have been found in Protestant families and the interpretative in Catholic is something the historian and the sociologist can between them determine; but no one denies that it was so. And if the directors all happened to come from Ascendancy families, still there were degrees of snobbery within the Ascendancy. The Synges had lost their land and come down in the world, and I doubt if the Persses and Gregorys would have been willing to recognise as social equals the Yeatses or even the Pollexfens.

Lady Gregory used her social position to make the Abbey the moneyed friends it so much needed, and to get the stalls filled, and Willie Fay has recorded with gratitude how much they were helped by her 'genius for entertainment' and her first-night suppers on the stage. Even more did they relish the green-room teas, of which the mainstay was the famous barmbrack, a fruit-loaf of immense richness, weighing twenty-five pounds, which was (and still is) made by Gillan's bakery in the square at Gort.

In later years, when the Abbey players were prosperous and half of them had an eye on Hollywood, Lady Gregory's barmbracks were sometimes laughed at, and sometimes resented as a form of lady-of-the-manor patronage. But the heavy food parcels with which she toiled up to Dublin from Gort were no more patronage than were the hampers of good things she sent to Yeats in London, or to the Lanes and the Frank Persses in their leaner days. She knew how tiny were the salaries that were all the early Abbey could afford; one of

Sara Allgood's contracts was for 15s. a week. Of the directors, she was the one who worried because they could not keep up a professional standing on what they were paid, indeed could hardly be said to exist. She suspected they were underfed, and so, no doubt, they often were. The barmbracks and the chicken pies were her way of sharing with them her own very modest prosperity; one thinks, not of Lady Catherine de Bourgh, but of Colette's mother, demanding of any new arrivals in the village, *Est-ce que ces gens ont à manger chez eux?*

Her headquarters in Dublin were rented rooms in a private hotel in Nassau Street, and her description of the little feasts she would provide there after the night's work does not suggest any discrimination between 'gentlemen' and 'players'. 'My own meals were simple enough in that occupied Dublin time, but I would have on my table in the evening some provision of cold fowl or eggs or game, for there were no eating-houses open after theatre time, and Yeats and Synge and Fay, or some other artist, would find comfort in that simple meal.' Wherever she was, she made a little aura of welcome and good food.

Mr Gerard Fay has no record of his father or his uncle having stayed at Coole, but that was quite probably because they were too busy. Both of them were, by their own doing, savagely overworked during their Abbey years. Sara Allgood certainly stayed there many times as an honoured guest and so did other Abbey actors. But the gift of close intimacy was reserved for fellow-dramatists.

The change at the Abbey which resulted in paying the actors was made, I am certain, not from any desire on the part of Yeats or Lady Gregory to increase their power, but from their concern at exploiting people who could ill afford to give their services for nothing. Even so it was immediately resented by a group, headed by Maire nic Shiubhlaigh, who were not willing to continue in the position of dependants. They resigned, although agreeing to stay on long enough to see *The White Cockade* through.

4

The play is folk-history's version of James II's escape from Ireland after the battle of the Boyne, and in it she makes another of those astonishing strides forward, into complete control of her material. It is one of her two best full-length plays, the one of which Synge said that 'it had made the writing of historical drama again possible'. There was no cavilling from Yeats this time; he told Symons: 'Lady Gregory has done a very original play, at once merry and beautiful.' The only dissentient voice appears to have been Willie Fay's, who found in it a diffuseness of action which made it difficult to produce.

I fail to understand why. The theme is strong and consistent; it is loyalty, loyalty to Ireland, focussed (unworthily as it turns out) on the shrinking figure of King James. It is personified by Sarsfield, James's heroic general, and by the half-mad Old Lady who has given up all for the Stuart cause.

It is true that James and Sarsfield do not appear in the first scene, but they are talked of, and we become very quickly aware that this inn kitchen is the place where they will take refuge, and that one of the dramas then to be played out will lie in the soul of young Owen Kelleher, the son of the house. He is the adolescent at the fork in the road. His life can become pointless, like his drunken father's and his grasping mother's, or it can amount to something. The triumph or the defeat of loyalty will be expressed in him.

The specious Mrs Kelleher with her eye to the main chance is brilliantly drawn. She speaks entirely in catchwords and proverbs without ever stepping beyond the sense of her part — a bravura feat comparable to George Eliot's Mrs Poyser.

Listen to her meeting her match in the Williamite sergeant who is determined to billet his men on her inn:

Mrs Kelleher: A hen itself is heavy if you carry it far. It's best to give up in time. A good run is better than a bad battle. We got no comfort for ourselves — what is nearest the church is not nearest the altar.

Sergeant: Quiet this woman, some of you. Where is the man of the house? The hen doesn't crow when there is a cock in the yard — you see, ma'am, I have proverbs myself.

He gets his way and billets himself and a trooper, and when James and Sarsfield, led by Owen, arrive after the defeat at the Boyne, they find they have walked into a trap.

Then follows one of the best scenes Lady Gregory ever wrote, a scene closely parallel to the more famous one of the sergeant's conversion in *The Rising of the Moon*, but richer and subtler, because Sarsfield's deadly-earnest game is being played on three levels. First, he is pretending to be the King, while the real King sits huddled with averted face on the far side of the table; then, he is appealing to the two soldiers to let their King escape; but most important of all to himself and to the audience, he is appealing over their heads to James, striving to rouse in James something of his own heroic spirit, begging him to stay and make another stand instead of fleeing to France.

Owen: It must be a wonderful thing to be a king!

Sarsfield: Wonderful indeed — if he have the heart of a king — to be the son and grandson and great-grandson of kings, the chosen and anointed of God. To have that royal blood coming from far off, from some source so high that like the water of his palace fountain it keeps breaking, ever breaking away from the common earth, starting up as if to reach the skies. How else would those who are not noble know when they meet it what is royal blood?

1st Williamite: I would know in any place that this King has royal blood.

2nd Williamite: It is easy to see among these three which of them is King.

Sarsfield (looking at James): A wonderful thing! If he have the high power of a King, or if he take the counsel that should be taken by a King. To be a King is to be a lover — a good lover of a beautiful sweetheart.

1st Williamite: I suppose he means the country, saying that.

2nd Williamite: I am sure he must have a heart for Ireland. . . .

Sarsfield: If she is in trouble or under sorrow, this sweetheart who trusts him, that trouble, God forgive him, brings him a sort of joy! To go out, to call his men, to give out shouts because the time has come to show what her strong lover can do for her — to go hungry that she may be fed; to go tired that her dear feet may tread safely; to die, it may be, at the last for her with such glory that the name he leaves with her is better than any living love, because he has been faithful, faithful, faithful!

1st Williamite (putting down his musket): I give up the Dutchman's pay. This man is the best. . . .

2nd Williamite: We will fight for you five times better than ever we fought for the Dutchman. We will not let so much as a scratch on one belonging to you — even that lean-jawed little priest at the end of the table, (pointing at James).

Sarsfield (rising): That is right. I knew you were good Irishmen. Now we must set out for Clonmel.

James: No, no, we cannot go. We must wait for the men from the French ship.

James is allowably treated as a figure of comedy, from the opening ding-dong dialogue between himself and his secretary when they are planning to evade the too zealous devotion of their general, to his final attempt at escape in a barrel, upon which folk-history insists. He is no villain opposed to Sarsfield's shining flame; his are merely the pathetic scuttlings and schemings of the small man caught up in events too large for his capacity. He gets away, leaving his 'beautiful sweetheart' to the vengeance of the conqueror.

And so all fails. Owen loses his private battle of the Boyne, and returns, disillusioned, to his life of idleness. The Old Lady retreats deeper into her world of fantasy. Only Sarsfield is left, to buckle on his sword again for the cause that transcends King James, the cause that is after all something within himself. This last, most moving scene crowns what is to my mind a little masterpiece, worthy to stand beside the earlier plays of her friend Bernard Shaw, and not so unlike them in its rueful homely idealism. Sarsfield has much in common with the Lavinia of *Androcles*, who discovers at the end that she is willing to die 'for nothing'.

5

Each of the folk-history plays attempts something different. *Kincora* is epic, *The White Cockade* comedy, *Dervorgilla* tragedy. In *The Canavans* she has written what might be called a folk-farce, on the theme that 'Queen Elizabeth was awful'. Folk-history made Queen Elizabeth come into Ireland and display her awfulness at first hand, but Lady Gregory does not go so far; the Queen is merely impersonated in her play. Like all pieces that rely on disguise for their main effect, it reads disappointingly, but she assures us that 'it acts very merrily', and it is the only full-length play of hers that has had a comparatively recent revival. Perhaps 'scandal about Queen Elizabeth' still has a strong Irish appeal.

In *Dervorgilla* she returns to the one-act form for a tragedy of remorse. Dervorgilla is the woman on whom folk-history lays the blame for bringing the English into Ireland. The wife of one Irish provincial king, she was stolen away, willingly or unwillingly, by another, and her husband invaded her lover's province; Henry II of England was appealed to, and sent over the army under Strongbow which never again left.

In the play, Dervorgilla is an aged woman who has outlived husband and lover, but not the trouble she has brought on her country. Alone at the Abbey of Mellifont, her identity known only to her two faithful servants, she strives by ceaseless

H

prayer and sacrifice to atone. She is persuaded to come outside the walls, where the children are running races and showing off their handicrafts, and in a charming little scene she makes friends with them and gives them prizes. But a wandering poet arrives, with a song about Dervorgilla the wicked queen, and a shadow is cast over the sunny day; and then a drunken English bowman wantonly shoots the old man, Dervorgilla's servant, and in her grief his wife blurts out the truth. The children know nothing of the rights and wrongs of the case beyond what they have heard the poet sing, but one by one they creep sadly back and return their prizes.

'Do not be afraid to give back my gifts,' says Dervorgilla to the last of them, 'do not separate yourself from your companions for my sake. For there is little of my life but is spent, and there has come upon me this day all the pain of the world and its anguish, seeing and knowing that a deed once done has no undoing, and the lasting trouble my unfaithfulness has brought upon you and your children for ever. There is kindness in your unkindness, not leaving me to go and face Michael and the Scales of Judgment wrapped in comfortable words, and the praises of the poor, and the lulling of psalms, but from the swift, unflinching, terrible judgment of the young!'

There is a spaciousness, an elegiac nobility about *Dervorgilla* which sets it apart from the other, more intimate one-act tragedies, *The Gaol Gate* and *MacDonough's Wife*, and many consider it the finest of the three. At any rate it is flawless of its kind, and Sara Allgood's acting in the chief part made a deep impression, though she was a very young woman still. To have seen her play it at the height of her powers must have been an experience indeed.

Perhaps *The Deliverer* (1911) should also come under the heading of folk-history; in it the Jewish mob's treatment of Moses is used as an allegory of the Irish mob's treatment of Parnell. The shadowy figure of 'the king's nurseling' bears little resemblance to either Moses or Parnell, but the mob is very recognisable, and by no means exclusively Irish, in its fickleness, cruelty and hysteria. An eerie little piece, too tenuous perhaps to hold the stage, but with something about it that lingers in the mind.

6

Dervorgilla was the last of Lady Gregory's plays to be produced by the Fays, or at any rate her last acknowledged play, for it was immediately followed by *The Unicorn from the Stars*, the Yeats fantasy which, as he himself has stated, was to all intents and purposes hers.

For two years Miss Horniman had been intensifying her campaign against the Fays, and by the end of 1906 she had succeeded to the point where an Englishman, Ben Iden Payne, was brought in as co-producer. The move was bitterly opposed by both Lady Gregory and Synge, who knew well how much their plays owed to the two brothers; indeed, Lady Gregory says in *Our Irish Theatre* that she never agreed to it, but that her letter of opposition lay uncollected for a fortnight during snowy weather at Kiltartan, and Yeats took it that silence meant consent.

However, Willie Fay was still to produce the 'peasant' plays, while Payne took over the 'poetic' ones, which included, of course, the all-important plays of Yeats. The next thing that Miss Horniman heard was that the revival of *The King's Threshold* was still being produced by Willie Fay. Small wonder that she was furious. She paid the piper, but the Irish ranks had closed against her — as they were, needless to say, already closing against the unfortunate English producer — and never could she effectively succeed in calling the tune.

Payne found his position untenable and after six months resigned, though his later career in England, partly under Miss Horniman herself, was to show him as a producer of great gifts. Willie Fay then seems to have seen his opportunity to get rid of rival and directors too. He demanded a reinforcement of his authority which would have given him back most of the powers he held before the directorship was formed.

The directors had fought for him against the tyranny of Miss Horniman, but they would not let him become a tyrant in his turn. They had no notion of dismissing him; on the contrary, Yeats's memorandum on the reorganisation of the theatre shows that one of their objects was to spare him drudgery and free him for more artistic work. But after the meeting at which they had discussed his demands, he writes, 'Lady Gregory came to me to say that they were not disposed to make any changes, and what was I going to do about it? I did the only thing that was left to me — I resigned on the spot.'

Lady Gregory, it seems clear, was acting as messenger for her fellow-directors, but the understandable bitterness of the Fays over their banishment (even if it was self-banishment) from their own theatre was chiefly directed against her, who had been their most consistent champion. Fortunately, she does not seem to have known of it. Her references to them, both then and later, are always appreciative.

Against their real enemy, Miss Horniman, neither of them ever uttered a word of complaint. Mr Gerard Fay can find no explanation beyond the wellnigh unbelievable one that they did not know she had been attacking them, (nor, one must equally infer, that Lady Gregory had been defending them). Willie Fay says somewhere in his book that the life of a strolling player develops ability to judge character. One can only conclude that in this branch of his professional equipment he would seem to have got off to a slow start.

VII

'Collaboration' — Yeats

All literary collaboration is a mystery; but in the case of the Abbey dramatists it is less mysterious than usual because they — and particularly Lady Gregory — have left clear indications of the ways in which they helped and were helped. Nevertheless, by disregarding these, waiting till she was dead, and then trapping Yeats into the condoning of misstatements in his old age, a group of Dublin literary gossips headed by the egregious Oliver St John Gogarty succeeded in completely distorting the picture. Their efforts, which as far as I can make out passed pretty well unchallenged in an anti-feminist country, have subjected Lady Gregory's reputation to an injustice as outrageous as any that literary history can show.

She is attacked on two counts, which at first glance would seem to be mutually contradictory: that she interfered with and spoilt Yeats's plays, and that he really wrote the best of hers.

For the first charge there is some justification, though the blame lies entirely with Yeats, who demanded her help; for the second there is none whatever.

We have already seen how Yeats acknowledged his indebtedness over *Kathleen ni Houlihan*. In his note to *The Pot of Broth* he is even more specific:

'I hardly know how much of the play is my work, for Lady Gregory helped me as she has helped in every play of mine where there is dialect, and sometimes where there is not. In these first years of the Theatre we all helped one another with plots, ideas and dialogue, but certainly I was the most indebted as I had no mastery of speech that purported to be of real life.'

Lady Gregory in *Our Irish Theatre* summarises her share in his plays thus:

'I began by writing bits of dialogue, when wanted. Mr Yeats used to dictate parts of *Diarmuid and Grania* to me, and I would suggest a sentence here and there. Then I, as well as another, helped to fill in the spaces in *Where There is Nothing*. Later in the year we wrote together *Kathleen ni Houlihan*. For *The Pot of Broth* I also wrote dialogue and I worked as well at the plot and the construction of some of the poetic plays, especially *The King's Threshold* and *Deirdre*; for I had learnt by this time a good deal about play-writing, to which I had never given thought before.'

Moore having failed as a dramatic collaborator, Yeats turned to Lady Gregory; but why did he need a collaborator at all? Why this failure of confidence in one so arrogantly certain of himself in every other field? Obviously, because he was going against the grain of his genius. It was the genius of the lyric, not the dramatic, poet, and it is possible to hold with his biographer, J. M. Hone, that in diverting it to the service of the Irish dramatic revival he was showing considerable unselfishness.

The lyric genius finds all within itself, the dramatic looks outward. Very rarely are the two combined, as in Shakespeare or Goethe. More commonly the lyric poet, Shelley, Browning, Tennyson, scores a brave near-miss with a play which has cost him an agony of effort. *I who have never observed anything, or listened with an attentive ear, but value all I have seen and heard because of the emotions they call up, or because of something they remind me of that exists, as I believe, beyond the world.* . . . In that stately piece of self-criticism, Yeats had put his finger on what it was that inhibited him when he came to write his plays.

Aware that he was on a false trail, he groped towards a sort of tragedy which should not require those gifts of observation and human sympathy in which he was lacking. 'Tragedy is passion alone, and rejecting character, it gets form from motives, from the wandering of passion; while comedy is the clash of character. . . . In practice most works are mixed: Shakespeare being tragi-comedy.' He finds support for this theory in the tragedy of Greece and Rome, (where, however, it partook of a religious rite), and in that of Corneille and Racine. In this last example he is unfortunate. No one who has read Racine with more than cursory attention could suppose that his persons lack character, or would be unable to differentiate between jealousy as expressed by Phèdre, and jealousy as expressed by Roxane.

Applied to the modern theatre as most of us understand it, the theory is surely nonsense. Great tragedy certainly 'universalises' character, but then so does great comedy. The persons of a play must be real as individuals before they can be real as types and symbols; to take a short-cut to the symbol will answer for a lyric writer, but not for a dramatic one. What matters, both for tragedy and for comedy, is to avoid *triviality* of character, the detail that raises the facile tear and the cheap laugh; that is what is wrong with second-rate dramatic writing, and what the Abbey group headed by Yeats were out to combat. The dramatist must seize on the detail that is revealing and significant — and no amount of theory can teach him how to do that.

The theory of character-rejecting tragedy will hold, however, for the sort of drama Yeats was equipped to write, the poetic meditation cast in dramatic form, like Milton's *Comus* or Shelley's *Prometheus*. And such works, if of the highest quality, command a specialised audience. Many of Yeats's plays, and particularly the exquisite dirge that is his *Deirdre*, will always be heard with pleasure, though perhaps they are better suited to sound radio than to the stage.

What Yeats needed was the courage of his convictions, to persevere on his own course and let plot and character go hang; but what the Abbey needed in those anxious early years was the play that would fill the house. Accordingly he called in his closest friend, who had the common touch. One is reminded of Miss Compton-Burnett's would-be novelist, who went through the draft of his manuscript 'putting in the charm'.

It worked in the case of *Kathleen*, because an abstract central character can carry a one-act play, if it is an abstraction — in this case the liberation of Ireland — to which the audience will respond. But in the longer plays, the Yeatsian abstraction weighs like lead upon the mercurial Gregory minor characters; each shows up the weak points of the other, they will not fuse.

There is, moreover, a sacerdotal and didactic element in Yeats, a quality which, while it made him a great literary leader, is essentially anti-dramatic. We are continually being lectured and 'got at' on behalf of some high ulterior motive or symbolic meaning. The central situation of *The King's Threshold*, the poet on hunger-strike, is in itself exciting (it was in fact later copied by real life). But Seanchan is not a real person dying of hunger; he is a mouthpiece, giving us Yeats's views on the function of the artist in politics.

For successful collaboration, we must presuppose a general resemblance in the cast of the collaborating minds. If they are writing a play, one may perhaps excel at plot and construction and the other at character and dialogue, but both must have a dramatic bias. Lady Gregory could collaborate with Hyde, because he already possessed the two basic attributes of the dramatist, an interest in people and a gift for writing easy, natural dialogue, at any rate in Irish. But Yeats she could only patch, because his talent was essentially solitary and indrawn. As an organising team they were superb, but as a creating team they were temperamentally at cross-purposes. Yeats's admirers are in the main right to see her as more hindrance than help, and to find a fuller expression of his genius in his later plays, written alone, and when he had abandoned all hope of a popular stage success, or indeed of any stage presentation.

So much I concede; but what they have signally failed to acknowledge is that her attempts to make Yeats actable were equally a waste of her talent, and that she put precious material into his plays which could not benefit them and ought to have been saved for her own.

2

The outstanding example of such waste is the curious and exasperating *Unicorn from the Stars*, which began its dramatic life as *Where There is Nothing*, the play in which 'I, as well as another, helped to fill spaces'. Endlessly tinkered with, it was finally handed over to her by Yeats in disgust, and produced in its retitled version at the Abbey in November, 1907.

Yeats says of it that 'but for the fable and the chief character it is wholly her work'. But the fable and the chief character are just what is wrong with it. The chief character is Martin, a man in a trance, who comes out of it at intervals to deliver yet another instalment of a fairly high-falutin' sermon — this I suppose may be considered the fable. Together they constitute Yeats at his sacerdotal worst.

This would not signify if the rest were journeyman stuff. It is not, it is first-rate Gregory; she has seldom written with more human warmth. Martin is the son and nephew of coachbuilders, and Thomas, the father, is another of her splendid Dogberry figures:

Any person I will take in hand, I will make a clean job of them the same as I would make of any other thing in my yard — coach, half-coach, hackney-coach, ass-car, common-car, post-chaise; calash, chariot on two wheels, on four wheels. Each one has the

shape Thomas Hearne put on it; and what I can do with wood
and iron, why would I not be able to do it with flesh and blood,
and it in a way my own?

Equally real is Andrew, his feckless, superstitious brother.

Against Thomas's respectability is set a raffish band of
strolling beggar-players, savage characters which, Yeats says,
delighted him, and which strike a quite new, an almost
Syngean note in her work, with their quarrelling and cursing
— 'That the pain of your front tooth may be in your back
tooth, you to be grabbing my share!' — their charms and
spells and covetousness. There is a wonderful opening to the
last act, where Martin lies seemingly dead by the seashore (to
the audience's relief) and the two women of the band, half-
fearful and half-gloating, mull over the plunder of the great
house they have helped to burn down in the night.

To leave the big house burning after us, it was that crowned
all! Two houses to be burned to ashes in the one night. It is likely
the servant girls were rising from the feathers and the cocks
crowing from the rafters for seven miles around, taking the flame
to be the whitening of the dawn.

It is almost the same destructive ecstasy, amoral and joyous,
that we find in the gypsies of Synge, and the pity of it is that
she never pursued them over any other hill, never sounded
that particular eerie note again.

3

That W. B. Yeats could have written the plays of Lady
Gregory, when he felt himself so little of a natural dramatist
that he had to call her in to help him write his own, is on the
face of it absurd. But no rational objection of that sort
hampered the progress of Oliver St John Gogarty's smear-
campaign. *How much of her plays did she write? Yeats had spent
many months annually in collaboration with her at Coole Park.
I almost got him to acknowledge his authorship of 'The Rising of*

the Moon'. And so on. The fact that *As I was Going Down Sackville Street* is a highly readable book, original-seeming in its discursive style, too, to those who do not know *Ave*, gave these insinuations a currency well beyond Dublin.

The only evidence he could have adduced of Yeats's having had a hand in her plays — and as far as I know he did not adduce it, doubtless preferring to condemn her unread — is the dedication to Yeats of her first collected volume, the *Seven Short Plays*, 'because you have taught me my trade'.

It is the sort of gesture which should, I suggest, be taken only in the most general sense. In that sense, Yeats had taught all the Abbey dramatists their trade. His enthusiasm and confidence, his sense of the high seriousness of literature and his primary part in getting the theatre founded were the factors which had made it possible for the rest of them to write. He had also evolved an impressive body of dramatic theory, though as I have pointed out, it was a theory which only in effect applied to his own work.

But the implication that he 'taught' her in the sense of showing her how to write plays is directly contradicted by the statements of both of them that she worked on the plots and construction of his poetic plays, 'for I had learned by this time a good deal about playwriting.' If she had learned it from *him*, he would have had no need to summon her aid.

He was interested in her work at the beginning, but his own always came first, both in his estimation and in hers. He had his own writing-room at Coole, at first the library, and after Robert's marriage a specially equipped bedroom, and it was sacred. That his hostess should have intruded on him with demands for help is unthinkable, though he might on occasion intrude on her. Her *Journals* prove that in later years he had no idea even of the subject of her plays until they were written; this was probably to a large extent true in the early years also.

He was a judicious critic, but in the nature of things a

mainly destructive one. He could tell her what was wrong
with a play, but he could not tell her how to set it right. For
that, she needed to turn to a natural dramatist. Synge could
have helped her had they been closer friends, and had he
himself not been working under pressure of anxiety and ill-
health; in later years Lennox Robinson supplied a vitalising
hint. But for the most part hers was a lonely struggle.

She herself delights to give us, in the notes to each play, the
seed from which it germinated in her mind. She is also
scrupulous about acknowledging direct help from another
writer. Only one such acknowledgment is made to Yeats, in
the notes to *The Travelling Man*, and that is really an excess of
candour, since we know from *Our Irish Theatre* and from his
letters that the original idea had been hers (in any case it is a
legend as old as folklore), and that he had taken it from her,
worked on it, been dissatisfied and thrown it back. Nor is it
among her happiest, being too directly a sermon — perhaps
Yeats' didacticism coming through.

But it is *The Rising of the Moon* that calumny is most
determined to attribute to Yeats, for the single reason that it
is her big success. It is revived not merely oftener than her
other plays, but ten times oftener. It is the only work of hers
many people know, and it has given its title and the skeleton
of its plot to an Irish triple-story film.

The sweeping of the board by a playlet which, though
delightful, is slight compared with much else she wrote is as
saddening in its way as the success of Yeats's 'Lake Isle of
Innisfree', but there is nothing mysterious about it. It is an
experience which befalls most writers, certainly most writers
of fiction, whether in novel or dramatic form. One book or
play catches the mass fancy as nothing else before or after it.
It is seldom the best, or even the one over which we have
worked hardest. It is simply the lucky one; luck sat on our
shoulders as we wrote.

The appeal of *The Rising* is easy to understand. To the swiftness of action she had already achieved in village comedies like *Spreading the News* (and which the stately Yeats never achieved anywhere) she adds a 'rebelly' flavour which strikes instant echoes in the Irish soul. Night on the quays, the man on the run, the police-hunt, the sergeant torn by conflicting loyalties — it is sure-fire stuff. There is about it a tingle of excitement which, I must concede, she never quite caught again. But excitement is not everything. The great act of *The White Cockade* has nearly the same tension, with a subtler development of character, and in her other one-act masterpieces, *The Workhouse Ward* and *The Gaol Gate*, irony and poignancy take its place.

It is also perfectly easy to see where *The Rising* comes from. Of some of her plays, one thinks wonderingly: Now how on earth can she have known that? But this one is Gregory to a positively autobiographical extent. The Fenian troubles had been avidly followed in the nursery at Roxborough. The conflict in the sergeant's mind is the conflict in the mind of the child, receiving downstairs 'the strict Orangism of the drawing-room', and upstairs the imperfectly concealed rebel sentiments of old Mary Sheridan. All the mature playwright has to do is to transform the child's age, sex and social class, a simple process to any competent writer of fiction, and there the sergeant stands. Mary Sheridan's story of Hamilton Rowan and his escape by boat supplies the rest of the plot.

And if there are still persons who believe that they can see the hand of W. B. Yeats in any of this, then I am driven to the Wellingtonian conclusion that they will believe anything.

4

Confidence is an essential attribute of any writer of fiction. The whole process is a confidence-trick. To create a world of lifelike men and women, and impose it on the reader or on the audience, requires an enormous amount of sheer nerve. Anything that weakens that nerve, weakens the creative force. That is why writers seldom benefit from even justified criticism if it is purely negative. I think it is Mr J. B. Priestley who with his usual honesty has said: 'The man who tells me I can't write aims a pistol at my heart.'

Failure of nerve is a malady to which women writers are peculiarly prone. One senses it frequently in George Eliot, with whom Lady Gregory has a good deal in common. For chapter after chapter she will sail along her tight-rope over the morass, and then suddenly, for no apparent reason, she wavers, she falls. Into coincidence, into cliché, into manufactured situations such as the lover seeing the faithful mistress in the arms of another and concluding the worst, (for example the unconvincing misunderstanding between Ladislaw and Dorothea towards the end of *Middlemarch*). George Eliot had been fortunate in acquiring for life the most loyal of literary comrades, always ready to buttress up her failing confidence; but even so, she sometimes falls.

And here (in case I should be accused of feminist *parti-pris*) is the opinion of a man, and a dramatist of the first order, on the situation between Yeats and Lady Gregory over the writing of *Kincora*:

'Give it up! No wonder it wasn't the success it might have been. Why didn't Yeats mind his own business! A pity the woman was so near to Yeats while she was writing the play: he had a bad effect on her confidence in her own creation. She was concerned with him and her play; he concerned only with himself. He had no right to tell her to give up writing the play; but she served so frequently in so many common ways that Yeats easily dismissed from his mind her natural vigour in the creation of imaginative drama.'

So in his honest indignation speaks Sean O'Casey, who knew well just how much harm failure of nerve can do. He goes on to attribute some of Lady Gregory's weaknesses to her being overburdened with the work of others and therefore writing in too much of a hurry, but I am not quite with him there. She often wrote best when she wrote fastest — *The Gaol Gate*, for instance, or *MacDonough's Wife* — and she always wrote conscientiously, putting good workmanship into everything she did. If a play would not 'come right' she tussled and tinkered with it tirelessly. Her failures are never, it seems to me, the result of hurrying or skimping; they are failures of nerve. If it is generally true that she does better in the one-act than in the three-act form, still there is *The White Cockade* to prove that she had it in her to write full-length plays. But too often thereafter, one feels that she is defeated before she begins.

It would manifestly be unfair to lay all this at Yeats's door, but it seems as plain to me as it did to Sean O'Casey that he must take part of the blame. They were comrades and equals, and his speaking his full mind to her was in the general sense a stimulus, and may be held to have increased her confidence; but over specific pieces of work, his attitude of negative criticism and deflation did her harm. It was no one-sided process; on occasion, as her letters show, she could round on him and tell him that a poem was inferior or obscure. But I do not suppose that she ever succeeded in frightening him, whereas he constantly, whether or not he intended it, frightened her.

Would she have done better without him? Would she have done anything without him? It is the sort of human sum that can never be added up with certainty; there are too many imponderables. She would certainly not have chosen to be without him, though the implication that she was in the literary sense his creature is one I hope I have already disproved. By and large he probably gave her more than he took away.

VIII

'Collaboration' — Hyde and Synge

Douglas Hyde had no ambition to be a playwright. His literary gift was lyric, and expressed itself in his Irish poems; but in any case the Gaelic League was the principal interest of his life. He wrote his Irish plays to further the popularity of the revived language, and to give material to the amateur actors at the local *feis*. Plot and characters were supplied to him by Lady Gregory, in the form of what she calls a 'scenario'; all he had to do was to write the dialogue, for which he had a racy aptitude.

She credits Yeats with supplying the plot of *The Twisting of the Rope*, but as we have seen, it was a folktale Hyde knew already; also with 'giving its shape' to the legend of *The Lost Saint*, but knowing the difficulty Yeats found in constructing his own plays, we may be fairly certain that she in fact constructed Hyde's. The plays were chiefly written at Coole, and *The Marriage* and *The Poorhouse* come direct from her. Yeats in *Dramatis Personae* has left a charming description of Hyde scribbling away at his desk all morning, with a facility the other two envied, and then being drawn away by Lady Gregory for an afternoon's fishing on the lake.

Once again, there is no mystery about any of this. Hyde's own statements, and the 'Play-writing' chapter of *Our Irish Theatre*, make it perfectly clear. Nevertheless another section of the Dublin literary world clings to the belief that the debt was from Lady Gregory to Hyde and not *vice versa*; in particular, it credits him with her second most successful one-acter, *The Workhouse Ward*. There is no malice in this error, as there is in the attribution of *The Rising of the Moon* to Yeats, but it persists, and is part of the process of nibbling Lady Gregory's credit away.

The genesis of *The Workhouse Ward* is plain to anyone who troubles to read that chapter. The notion of the two old people kept alive by their joy in a quarrel was given to Lady Gregory by an incident in Gort Workhouse. She outlined it to Yeats, but he decided that another Gaelic play was what was needed at that juncture, and 'rather sadly' she was compelled to hand her brain-child over to Hyde. The 'scenario' which she supplied to him is reproduced in full, and it is a play step by step complete except for the actual words of the characters.

Hyde followed it without alteration, and the result was *Tigh na mBocht*, translated back into English by her as *The Poorhouse*. I do not, alas, read Gaelic, but the texts of the two versions have survived in the Abbey's journal *Samhain*, and from the English one it can be seen how faithfully he has retained her scaffolding.

It is a gently amusing little play, but when put on, it proved too diffuse and had too many characters. There is a Matron who is superfluous, and there are other half-seen old men to whom the two quarrellers address a good part of their remarks. These faults, of course, were Lady Gregory's own.

She remained dissatisfied, and a year later, 'with Dr Hyde's full leave', she took back her story and rewrote it as *The Workhouse Ward*. It is a complete re-casting. Not only is it now pruned to the three essential characters, the two old men and the sister who brings the offer of release to one of them; the dialogue, the quarrelling, are brand-new. Hyde's points in dispute were funny in a conventional way; Lady Gregory's are infinitely more varied, ramified and colourful, more wounding and insulting, more impregnated with family

I

pride and snobbery, with boasts of the numbers of cars at funerals, and of those for whom the banshee wails. Comparison of the two texts is instructive; nothing reveals more clearly how Lady Gregory's classic talent, when she is at the top of her form, can lift an anecdote from the particular to the universal.

This quality in the play was at once recognised and it was hailed as a symbol of divided Ireland — 'that most subtly national and topical of one-act plays', Micheal MacLiammoir has called it. Authors are, of course, always enchanted to have symbolic meanings discovered in their works, and Lady Gregory was no exception. But I do not for a moment believe that she deliberately set out to personify the Irish troubles in her two old men. It is because they are sharply real and individualised on their own ground, the ward of Gort Workhouse, that they are true on a national and indeed a universal level, and that they will go on throwing their pillows at each other to the end of time.

The Workhouse Ward is thus, I trust, indisputably established as Lady Gregory's own. Certainly no one would have been more distressed than the gentle and golden-hearted author of *The Poorhouse* that injustice should be done to her on his account.

Of the plays which represent a genuine collaboration between them, *The Marriage* seems to me the most delightful. She based it on one of the stories she was told about the blind poet Raftery, how he came to a cottage where two young people were marrying in dire poverty, and by his songs and laughter 'made a feast where no feast was'. She has turned it into a ghost-story, a form not only more dramatic but better suited to Hyde's gift for evocative other-worldly speech, and as the event proved, to his acting powers too. It was first given at the Galway Feis of 1902, and, the principal player falling out at the last minute, Hyde himself was persuaded to take the part. She has left her record of the effect he made. 'It will be hard to forget the blind poet, as he was represented on the stage by the living poet, so full of kindly humour, of humorous malice, of dignity under his poor clothing, or the wistful ghostly sigh with which he went out of the door at the end.'

After *The Poorhouse* Hyde wrote no more plays, and the rest of his life was frustrating, with the Gaelic League becoming more and more a political instrument in spite of all he could do to check it. Nor did the language revival produce the social and spiritual results of which he had dreamed, and it is now regarded as a stultifying fetish by great numbers among the Irish themselves. The honour paid to him in his old age, when he was elected the first President of Ireland in 1938, can hardly have been compensation for such bitter disappointment.

If he had stayed by the side of his friend Augusta Gregory, had let his poetic and his latent dramatic gifts develop, might he not have left a more permanent memorial of that humanity and humour that all recognised? But creative talent, where it is genuinely present, is always an overriding taskmaster. In the case of Douglas Hyde, one can only regretfully conclude that it was not.

2

Synge, who pronounced that all art was collaboration, for practical purposes collaborated with nobody. Once he had received from Yeats the initial impetus to visit the Aran Islands, the development of his genius was a process as solitary and relentless as the beating of the Atlantic against the cliff of Dun Aengus. But two sufficiently striking acknowledgments he did make to Lady Gregory. When her *Cuchulain* came out, he told Yeats that he had found in it the dialect he had been trying to master, and he wrote to herself: 'Your

Cuchulain is part of my daily bread.' And in the notes to *The White Cockade*, she tells us that 'I was pleased to hear that J. M. Synge had said my method had made the writing of historical drama again possible'. Yeats's statement in *Dramatis Personae* that 'neither I nor Lady Gregory ever had a compliment from him' is therefore demonstrably untrue. What it means is, 'Synge did not praise my plays,' and a fair inference is that he did not praise them because he did not think they were good plays.

No one who was temperamentally an egotist could have entered as Synge did into human nature in all its diversity. His is pre-eminently the dramatist's temperament, listening, observing, recording, leading others on to talk rather than talking himself, and it makes a classic contrast with the lyric temperament of Yeats, whose life was a perpetual monologue, and a perpetual quest for the audience that should relieve him of the intolerable loneliness the nature of his genius imposed.

The researches of Professor David H. Greene, latest and most authoritative of the Synge biographers, based as they are on the personal recollections of his [Synge's] nephew Edward M. Stephens, have done a good deal to alter the picture of Synge as self-centred and morose. If he occasionally seemed so to his contemporaries, it was only towards the end, when he knew that his time was cruelly short. He was certainly not an intimate of Lady Gregory in the sense in which Yeats and Hyde were, for the good reason that he had little in the way of demands to make on her. He had no need of mothering, being already over-supplied with maternal solicitude; he had no need of encouragement, being driven by his own daemon; he had no need of plots. The picture drawn by Professor Greene bears out the account of their friendship which she gives in *Our Irish Theatre*: a steady liking between two people both of whom had important work on hand, and who were chiefly linked by their duties as co-directors of the theatre. It was possibly coloured on his side by a certain affectionate amusement, for to one of his immense sophistication she must always have seemed a trifle naïve.

They chiefly met in Dublin, or at her London parties while she kept on the Queen Anne's Mansions flat. Professor Greene has established that he only stayed at Coole five times, and only one of those visits (two weeks in 1904) was of any length. Indeed, it is difficult to imagine Coole making a deep appeal to one whose spirit was freed by the skeletal limestone landscape of Aran. The remark about 'civilisation in its most violent form', which nobody would remember if Lady Gregory herself had not recorded it, did not, however, apply to Coole, but to a 'somewhat warlike English lady' who was staying in the house — perhaps Miss Horniman? For Synge, the disadvantages of Coole could probably be summarised as too many trees, and too much Yeats.

His acknowledgment that Lady Gregory had shown him the dialect he had been trying to master is, in fact, a generous one, for his review of *Cuchulain of Muirthemne* in *The Speaker* of June 7th, 1902, proves his awareness that Hyde and others of the group had also been working towards the literary use of such a dialect:

'The intellectual movement that has been taking place in Ireland for the last twenty years has been developing a movement towards a nearer appreciation of the country people, and their language, so that it is not too much to say that the translation of the old manuscripts into their idiom is the result of an evolution rather than of a merely personal idea.'

What she probably did show him was that the country speech could be used for tragic and pathetic as well as comic purposes. It is significant that in this review he quotes in full Deirdre's lament over Naoise, which later he will himself paraphrase to such magnificent effect.

And of course the ultimate result, the prose-poetry of Synge's plays, is completely different from the 'Kiltartan' of Lady Gregory's. There is in this nothing surprising. Each writer of fiction takes from a dialect what suits his turn, even a relatively poor one such as Cockney showing great variations from author to author. Synge claimed that his dialogue was taken from life, and Professor Greene finds there is more truth in this claim than has generally been believed; there are direct borrowings in his plays from letters written to him by the Aran islanders, and from conversations he recorded verbatim in Kerry. The fact remains that no one peasant gathering could ever have spoken with the consistently rich imagery of the cast in a Synge play.

It has been tempting to some critics to bracket them together, and find Lady Gregory unrealistic too. And of course she has her favourite tricks of speech; certain of the Gaelic-based constructions particularly appeal to her for their neatness and elegance and she uses them more frequently than a real Gort citizen would; notably that subjunctive-infinitive which is almost her hallmark:

'It is a pity the banshee not to be crying for yourself'. 'It is no wonder a man to grow faint-hearted and he shut away from the light.' 'Is it a poor man like me, to have the name on him that he took a reward?'

(I have only found this 'Kiltartan infinitive' once in the plays of Synge, and that is in *Deirdre*, Act I, 'It is no work the High King to be slipping on stepping-stones,' where it may possibly have crept in through Lady Gregory's editing of the posthumous text.)

But those better fitted to judge of it than I am agree that by and large she gives a very faithful transcription of the speech of Gort and Loughrea. Micheal MacLiammoir, whose ear for accent and dialect is probably the most acute in Ireland, tells me that he overheard a new recruit to his company, of whose origins he knew nothing, talking in the green-room, and said to himself: that boy must come from East Galway, he talks like a Gregory character. The boy actually came from Kiltartan.

This is not in any sense to imply that the language of Lady Gregory is 'better' than that of Synge; considered as literature it is not anything like so varied and colourful. But in fact the comparison should not arise. Lady Gregory's language is right for her purpose, as Synge's is for his. The wild music of Synge would be as much out of place in the mouths of her characters as would the sonorous splendour of Yeats's verse. She has been set alongside them as part of the campaign of belittlement, instead of being judged by what she set out to do.

George Moore's gibes at the 'Kiltartan three-holed whistle' are therefore peculiarly pointless; he is demanding that the little fishes shall talk like whales. I have suggested that on the contrary, Lady Gregory is the natural complement to Synge; that the ear which can catch the charm of her gentle notes is all the better fitted to appreciate the thunder of his. So, after a week listening to the sea's surge and the gulls' crying along the cliffs of Inishmaan, does one return in contentment to the blackbirds and thrushes of the Coole lakeside, and even to the homely cackle of the poultry yard.

3

The main service rendered by Lady Gregory to Synge was a practical one. She fought, and bore the brunt of the fight, to get him a hearing.

She was quite as sincere a Nationalist as Maud Gonne, but she was determined that the dramatic movement should not be used as an instrument of political propaganda; for one thing, because she believed that most propagandist art is bad art, and for another, because it would inevitably have lost the Abbey the Ascendancy subscriptions on which it depended, and later the financial support of Miss Horniman.

It was Lady Gregory's duty, both as creative artist and as woman of affairs, to hold a middle course. She reaped the inevitable reward, of suspicion and vilification, often simultaneous, from both sides. To her own class she seemed a traitress, and to the Nationalists a blackleg. But it was chiefly Nationalist hostility she had to contend with up to the outbreak of the Civil War, and Ascendancy hostility thereafter. A less courageous woman would have been daunted by such many-angled unfairness. She did not enjoy it; she was not a 'born fighter' in the Maud Gonne sense; her letters and journals are full of her longing for the peace and 'charity with all men' so necessary to the creative writer. But she never wavered, and she never lost heart.

As she had seen it, the Abbey's surest way of helping in the struggle for liberty was to 'add dignity to Ireland'; but from the first, it was suspected in the Nationalist camp that this aspect of the dramatist's duty did not come uppermost with Synge. Maud Gonne and Arthur Griffith walked out of the first performance of The Shadow of the Glen in shocked protest — though one might really have expected Maud Gonne to be sympathetic towards another woman's struggle for personal freedom. By the time of the Playboy, it is clear, the Nationalists were gunning for Synge. Some kind of organised disturbance was pretty well foreseen — but Yeats went off to keep a lecture appointment in Scotland, Synge, already ill and hypersensitive, was in no fit state to do his own fighting, and Lady Gregory was the director on whom the impact fell.

The first night of the Playboy, January 26th, 1907, went off comparatively quietly till Christy reached the word 'shift', when the audience broke up in disorder, it being, one of them explained afterwards, a word a lady would blush to use even when she was alone.

By the second night, the Monday, the opposition had its

gang organised, and Lady Gregory noticed 'on one side of
the pit a large group of men sitting together, not a woman
among them'. Several accounts of this historic evening exist,
and Mr Gerard Fay in his book has gone minutely into them,
but there still seems no reason to doubt the version Lady
Gregory has given in *Our Irish Theatre*. She told Synge, she
says, about the group of men, 'and he telephoned to have the
police at hand.' Soon after the curtain rose the uproar began,
booings and tin trumpets drowning the actors' voices. Willie
Fay, who played Christy, stepped forward and appealed for
quiet. His nephew thinks it strange that neither of the directors
made the appeal, but Synge was ill and Lady Gregory had
never in her life spoken in public, nor could a woman's voice
have made itself heard where a man's failed; in any case the
gesture was easier for someone already on the stage.

But she was behind the policy. 'The curtain came down for
a minute, but I went round and told the actors to go on
playing to the end, even if not a word could be heard. The
police, hearing the uproar, began to file in, but I thought the
disturbers might tire themselves out if left alone, and I asked
them to go outside but stay within call in case of any attempt
being made to injure the players or the stage.' The disturbers
did not tire; nevertheless she was right to send the police out
again, for they were the symbol of British authority, and to
have accepted their protection would have been to brand the
Abbey as an Ascendancy theatre, and play right into the
Nationalists' hands.

Yeats returned and approved what she had done, and also,
it would seem, her alternative plan for protection, which was
to call in a nephew and his friends from Trinity College.
This, however, merely had the effect of turning a political
into a class struggle. The play was never properly heard till it
was given in Oxford and London in the summer, when it was
at once hailed as a masterpiece. In 1909 Dublin had a second

chance, and received it with 'very little opposition'. But the fame of the riots, and the play's value as a nuisance-making point to the Nationalist side, had crossed the Atlantic, and Lady Gregory was to fight its battle all over again in America.

Of course it was not primarily Synge she was fighting for; it was freedom of speech. 'We would not allow any part of our audience to make itself final judge through preventing others from hearing and judging for themselves. We have been justified, for Synge's name has gone round the world, and we should have been ashamed for ever if we had not insisted on a hearing for his most important work. But, had it been a far inferior play and written by some young writer who had never been heard of, we should have had to do the same thing. If we had been obliged to give in to such organised dictation, we should of necessity have closed the Theatre.'

For a time it was not only Nationalist opinion which was outraged by the *Playboy*, but some sections of Catholic opinion too. And this cost Lady Gregory what she personally valued far more than Dublin's approval, support on her home ground. Monsignor Fahy lost faith in her, and Blunt records in his diary for March 1907: 'At Gort, her county town, the local council has boycotted her, forbidding the schoolchildren to attend her teas and entertainments, lest their morals should be corrupted.' The embargo continued for several years and was a very real grief to Lady Gregory — and also, no doubt, to the schoolchildren and orphans.

It is good to know that the breach was healed. The principal achievement of the Vicar-General's last years (he died in 1919) was to put in hand the building of a fine new Catholic church; and Gort delights to tell a story that illustrates their warm yet wary friendship. The spire, though not the rest, was completed in Fahy's lifetime, and he took occasion to point out to Lady Gregory that it slightly over-topped that of the Protestant church. 'Yes, Monsignor,' she answered sweetly, 'but don't they both point in the same direction?'

4

In fact, she hated *The Playboy*.

Impossible to gloss over it, when she herself, always honest about her opinions, has gone out of her way to leave it on permanent record. She wrote to Hugh Lane from America: 'If you knew how I hate *Playboy* that I go out fighting for!' — and when she came to write his biography, this was a letter she elected to quote.

One's first reaction is of shock and disappointment, to find her siding in her heart with the Dublin mob. But this much can be said by way of defence: there is no indication that she 'hated' any other of Synge's plays. Admittedly she placed them below those of Yeats, but she had been among the earliest to recognise his quality, and she laboured with something like heroism at correlating the many versions of his posthumously produced *Deirdre*, and then at the actual production, 'through many snowy days and into winter nights until rheumatism seized me with a grip I have never shaken off.' She could justly claim: 'we have done our best for Synge's work since we lost him, as we did while he was with us here.'

Why, then, did she hate the *Playboy*? It matters to know, because of the light it throws on her own literary approach. She had to a remarkable extent managed to overcome her social background and upbringing and eradicate the lady-of-the-manor attitude, but something of the Roxborough social-worker remained with her always; her own kind-heartedness saw to that. Fundamentally she is a moral writer; equally fundamentally, Synge is an amoral one. This quality in him comes out most insistently in the *Playboy*; through it there runs a sinister little streak of cruelty, which is precisely what gives it its depth and fascination. And therefore she hated it, as a good many cultivated and sensitive people, particularly in Ireland, do to this day.

Of course it is comical cruelty; there is nothing in the absurd little 'torture-scene' of the last act to compare with the dreadful physical sufferings dragged on to the stage by the characters of O'Casey, the dramatist who made her 'glad to have been born'. But O'Casey is a moralist too; he is deploring and denouncing; he is filled with compassion and outrage. Synge is not, and that is the vital difference.

Synge was personally compassionate; his is not the amorality of the writer with no heart, which produces merely a literature of nastiness, but of the writer whose grasp is so wide that it must include the whole of human nature, good and bad, in one vast movement of comprehension and rejoicing. He cannot be constrained to take sides or to reform anyone or anything, for he would lose some essential if he did. Beauty is interpenetrated with desolation; kindliness co-exists with 'riot and severity and daring'; loneliness expresses itself in wild jests and laughter; the peasant who speaks with the voice of the ancient heroic world can hang a dog and find it funny. There is a chamber of horrors in every soul. We have far better reason to know this today than sixty years ago, when Synge was writing, yet it still has power to shock.

The word 'shock' is one that Synge himself constantly uses. He is a transmitter to us of the shocks that life gave him. 'There is hardly an hour that I am with them,' he writes of the Aran islanders, 'that I do not feel the shock of some inconceivable idea, and then again the shock of some vague emotion that is familiar to them and to me.' The picture he drew of the Aran islanders is in fact distorted, because he virtually omits the fervent religion that is the mainspring of their lives; but the picture he gives through them of humanity is valid and original. It is brand-new, with a child's freshness, yet we recognise it as a true picture, and that is why it shocks. Small wonder that a good many besides the Aran islanders were displeased with it, and that there is still something of a conspiracy to hush Synge up.

The contrast between his personal and his artistic attitude can be seen in the eerie train journey that closes the second part of *The Aran Islands*. The chivalrous Ascendancy gentleman watches over a shy young girl sitting beside him, but the artist has an ear cocked for the wit and brutality of the sailor in the compartment, and when the train stops, for the words of obscene songs being sung next door. And the innocence of the girl, the vitality of the blaspheming, drunken trainload are not really opposites. Each gains from the other, they are part of the whole that makes up 'the supreme beauty of the world'.

To this detachment — or it would be more accurate to say, to this complete involvement — Lady Gregory very rarely attains, and therefore it is hardly possible for her to sympathise with the extreme degree of it attained by Synge in *The Playboy*. Yet there are moments when she shakes off the ghost of the social worker. There is no right or wrong in the joyous quarrel of *The Workhouse Ward*, no blame allotted for the suffering and heartache of *The Gaol Gate* or *MacDonough's Wife*.

The amoral attitude is, I suspect, a particularly hard one for a woman writer to achieve, because her maternal function predisposes her towards benevolent interference, towards teaching and comforting and setting to rights. But Jane Austen seems to me one who achieves it over the greater part of her writing, even though morality with her is a surface dressing thickly spread. Jane Austen is not really deploring the vulgarity of Mrs Elton or the sadism of Mrs Norris, any more than Synge is deploring the violence of Pegeen Mike. She is rejoicing in the diversity of God's creatures, and whenever she forgets to do so and permits herself to take her sermon seriously, her spell is broken.

5

Something may here appropriately be said of Lady Gregory's friendship with Bernard Shaw. He was a friend to the theatre project from its early days, but his warm feeling for herself dated from another battle, over his play *The Shewing-Up of Blanco Posnet*, put on by the Abbey in 1909. It had been banned in England as blasphemous, but the Lord Chamberlain's jurisdiction did not extend to Ireland, and when Shaw offered it to them, Yeats and Lady Gregory jumped at the chance.

Miss Horniman had succeeded in ridding the theatre not only of the Fays, but of the producer who followed them, and the work was entrusted to Sara Allgood, who, however, found it altogether too much for her and appealed for help to Lady Gregory at Coole. Lady Gregory left for Dublin by the next train, and that evening took a rehearsal, the first she had ever taken alone. It was the discovery within herself of yet another talent. 'I thought out positions during the night, and next morning, when I had another rehearsal, I began to find an extraordinary interest and excitement in the work.' (From then on, she always had a hand in the production of her own plays, and often filled in the gaps between producers, though never very willingly; it took too much of her creative vitality, she found.)

Then Dublin Castle stirred. A letter from the Lord Lieutenant's office showed him prepared to take, in effect, upon himself the censorship functions of the English Lord Chamberlain. Lady Gregory as patentee of the theatre was threatened with loss of its patent if she allowed production of the play as it stood. She called on an official at the Castle, who asked that the 'blasphemous' expressions should be deleted;

she refused, explaining that the blasphemer's defiance of heaven constituted the subject of the play.

Next day Yeats arrived, and there were further interviews; her account of them in *Our Irish Theatre* reads like a page from one of her comedies. Finally, five days before the first performance was due, they were summoned to the presence of the Lord Lieutenant himself. Lord Aberdeen first saw Lady Gregory alone, possibly with a hope of appealing to class solidarity; if so he had come to the wrong aristocrat:

'Alas! — I must be discreet and that conversation with the King's representative must not be given to the world, at least by me. I can only mention external things: Mr. Yeats, until he joined the conference, being kept by the secretary, whether from poetical or political reasons, to the non-committal subject of spring flowers; my grieved but necessary contumacy; our joint and immovable contumacy; the courtesy shown to us and, I think, by us; the kindly offers of a cup of tea; the consuming desire for that tea after the dust of the railway journey all across Ireland; our heroic refusal, lest its acceptance should in any way, even if it did not weaken our resolve, compromise our principles. . . .'

They took counsel's opinion, which was that if they persisted in the face of a direct prohibition by the Crown, they exposed the theatre not only to loss of its patent but to a heavy fine. Four days later they heard from the Castle that such a prohibition would reach them immediately. The Abbey's few pounds of savings would be gone, and the players thrown out of work. They acknowledged defeat.

Then occurred one of the great moments of their organising collaboration, a proof that in matters of principle and policy their two minds were one mind, without need of words. They went down to the Abbey and carried on with the rehearsal, telling no one of their decision. And walking back through the lamplit streets afterwards, they found that independently they had both gone back on it. Their word had been given, 'at all risks we must keep it or it would never be trusted again'.

They sent to the papers a dignified statement to the effect that 'we must not, by accepting the English Censor's ruling, give away anything of the liberty of the Irish Theatre of the future'. *Blanco* was put on on the date announced, August 25th, 1909. Nothing untoward happened: 'perhaps the audience were waiting for the wicked bits to begin. Then, at the end, there was a tremendous burst of cheering, and we knew we had won.' The Castle's bluff was called.

Shaw was enchanted, and he rewarded Lady Gregory by an affection that was to last to the end of her life. He was not, once the glow of the *Blanco* victory had worn off, particularly attached to Yeats, but Lady Gregory evoked all that was most generous in his character. Respect for the staunch fighter was enhanced, in the creator of Candida, by a special sympathy for the woman of talent to whom was left so much of the donkey-work. Through all the dreary years of struggle over the Lane pictures, Ayot St Lawrence would be to her a haven, a place of encouragement when she was downhearted, of good food and fires and flowers, of good talk and good company. He read her excerpts from work in progress, and she suggested to him the page's sneeze which marks the turning of the wind in *St Joan*. There were many sides to G.B.S., and those who only knew the acrimonious egotist must have been surprised by her choice of adjective in her dedication of *The Golden Apple* 'to Bernard Shaw, the gentlest of my friends'.

6

I hope that I have justified the inverted commas of the headings to this and the previous chapter. I do not believe that there was ever, among the Abbey dramatists, collaboration in the Beaumont-and-Fletcher or Somerville-and-Ross sense. They helped each other, as Yeats says, with plots, ideas and dialogue, but it was a process in which Lady Gregory was far more creditor than debtor. This was not entirely due to her superior inventiveness; it also resulted from her being the principal translator of the group, and (as Hyde became more absorbed by his Gaelic League activities) its principal collector of folklore. It was she who had, or made, time to keep in touch with the country people, and to hear of daily happenings, as well as ancient legends, that would form the germ of plays.

It is a commonplace that genius is a bad friend to talent. Lady Gregory did her best work under a double shadow of genius, and in a sense it is astonishing that an elderly and self-educated woman was not thereby totally discouraged. She had her own, simpler, but supremely honest vision, and she held to it, remarkably uninfluenced by either Yeats or Synge. She served them as literary midwife and kitchenmaid when they needed her, and effaced herself when they did not. And it has been all too easy for those who never read her to conclude that she can have had nothing of importance to say herself.

As a woman writer, she had something definite and different to say, both in her comedies, and in her tragedies, which I will next consider.

IX

Tragedy

I

In her book *The Irish Dramatic Movement*, which is not only the best on its subject but contains the most thoughtful appreciation of Lady Gregory, the late Professor Una Ellis-Fermor represented Lady Gregory as subscribing to the theory of characterless tragedy put forward by Yeats. She found her support for this view in the lengthy note to *Damer's Gold*, all that has survived of a lecture on playwriting given by Lady Gregory in America.

And it certainly reads very like an echo of Yeats's doctrine. Tragedy, Lady Gregory told the women's clubs and the Vassar students, she had always found easier to write than comedy, because the tragic situation did so much more for the personages, and therefore the dramatist need do less.

'You may let your hero kick or struggle, but he is in the claws all the time, it is a mere question as to how nearly you will let him escape, and when you will allow the pounce. Fate itself is the protagonist, your actor cannot carry much character, it is out of place. You do not want to know the character of a wrestler you see trying his strength at a show.'

But this last, as a parallel, simply will not hold. The tragic protagonist is not to be equated with 'a wrestler you see trying his strength at a show'; if he were, then the heroes of film Westerns would be figures of tragedy, or the heroines strapped in the path of the oncoming train. The true tragic figure has brought at any rate a part of his disaster upon himself.

But if indeed Lady Gregory subscribed to Yeats's theory, then it is simply not borne out by her practice. She goes on to instance *The Gaol Gate* as a tragedy without character, a tragedy in which the persons are helplessly gripped by Fate. 'I made the scenario in three lines. *He is an informer, he is dead, he is hanged.* I wrote that play very quickly. My two poor women were in the clutch of the Woman in the Stars. I knew what I was going to do and I was able to keep within those three lines. But in comedy it is different, character comes in. . . .'

And in effect the two women are archetypal figures of tragedy, the wife and the mother of the man who is to die. She might therefore well have left them without character, relying simply on the pathos of their situation to move us. Whatever she may think herself, she has done nothing of the kind. The two women, within the brief frame of a one-act play, are not only individualised but contrasted, in their quite different reactions to calamity. The dour courage of the one, the pathetic gropings after comfort of the other, make them complete human beings, far removed from the single-quality poetic abstractions of Yeats.

The scene once again is the outside of Galway Gaol, that had so long haunted her imagination. Three boys from a mountain village (it is Derrykeel, the nearest hamlet to Chevy Chase) have been arrested for murder. Only against Denis is there positive evidence, though the whole village knows that Terry fired the shot. Now rumour has spread that Denis has informed against the other two and is to be freed, and a letter has come for Denis's wife and mother, which they, being illiterate, cannot read and are afraid to ask the neighbours to read for them. So they have journeyed through the night the terrible long road from Slieve Echtge to the gaol gate.

Young Mary is the tender, chicken-hearted wife; to have her Denis back in her arms is all she asks. 'It is no wonder a man to grow faint-hearted and he shut away from the light. I never would wonder at all at anything he might be driven to say.' But old Mary, though she loves her son deeply and frets over his health in the cold dark gaol, puts a good name above freedom. To be a murderer is one thing, but to be an informer — that is death in life. If indeed he has been promised his life on such terms, then he must live it in some other place. They will sell the holding, and he and his wife and child shall go to America, and she herself will end her days in some distant workhouse, remote from all who know of their dishonour. Young Mary has nothing of this heroic temper. The mere thought of leaving home fills her with terror. 'What person that is sent among strangers can have one day's comfort on earth?'

The gatekeeper comes out, reads their letter and breaks it to them that Denis died yesterday. 'To have died with his name under blemish,' the old woman cries, 'and left a great shame on his child!' To the young one, it is not the blemished name that matters, so much as the warm and living comrade gone. She breaks into a keen, so authentic that one turns up the translations in the *Kiltartan Poetry Book* to see if one of them has been used. But there is no copying here, simply a profoundly feminine re-interpretation of the ancient theme:

'What way will I be the Sunday, and I going up the hill to the Mass? Every woman with her own comrade, and Mary Cushin to be walking her lone!

'What way will I be the Monday and the neighbours turning their heads from the house? The turf Denis cut lying on the bog, and no well-wisher to bring it to the hearth!

'What way will I be in the night-time, and none but the dog calling after you? Two women to be mixing a cake, and not a man in the house to break it!

'What way will I sow the field, and no man to drive the furrow? The sheaf to be scattered before spring time that was brought together at the harvest!'

She begs her husband's body, and then the full truth
emerges. They cannot have the body because it lies in the
prison field. The unread letter was their summons to a last
meeting. He has been convicted of the murder, and hanged.
As there was no direct evidence brought against the other
two, they have been set free.

To the young woman, this is the last exacerbation of her
grief, and she meets it with wild curses. But to the old one, it
is the triumph of the spirit over the flesh. Denis was no
informer, he never spoke the word that would have saved
himself and implicated his friends. She spreads her hands and
shouts aloud, and the play ends on her paean of pride and
thanksgiving:

'Tell it out in the streets for the people to hear, Denis Cahel
from Slieve Echtge is dead. It was Denis Cahel from Daire-caol
that died in the place of his neighbour!

'It is he was young and comely and strong, the best reaper and
the best hurler. It was not a little thing for him to die, and he
protecting his neighbour!'

They typify eternally contrasted attitudes, these two; they
bear a distant relationship to Volumnia and Virgilia; but they
are not the less bewildered countrywomen from Derrykeel,
real figures in time and space, and in the history of a country
where solidarity against the oppressor has been the first duty
for seven centuries. They are among her most complete
creations and best acting parts, and to have seen the two
Allgood sisters, Sara and Molly (Maire O'Neill), interpret
them must have been to know the Abbey in one of the great
moments of its youth.

2

While there never was a time in Lady Gregory's connexion
with the Abbey when she could leave it to run itself and put
her own writing first, still Miss Horniman's support during

the first six years of its life and of her creative decade did mean that it was secure against financial shipwreck. But by the time she came to write her most important tragedy, the three-act, three-character *Grania*, there was no longer any such cushioning. This intense imaginative effort was not the fruit of leisure and solitude. A good part of her energies went back to the old wearisome task of raising funds to keep the theatre going.

Miss Horniman, inheriting another fortune on the death of her father, had founded in 1907 the project which became the Gaiety, Manchester, and transferred to it her main interest and all the ambitions that had been frustrated at the Abbey. She tried to transfer Yeats also, and failed, just as she had failed to galvanise him into taking what she considered the necessary steps to secure worthy production of his plays. The causes of her frustration were personified in Lady Gregory, who came first in her theatre and first with her friend, and who must have seemed to her to have emerged as a successful playwright at her expense. 'Lady Gregory,' wrote Yeats to Florence Farr in July of 1907, 'is now quite definitely added to Miss Horniman's list of truly wicked people.'

She prepared to cut her losses and relinquish her 'Irish toy', but on generous and dignified terms. Early in 1910 she offered to hand over the theatre to the directors (Lady Gregory and Yeats — Synge had died the year before) for a thousand pounds, which was only a fraction of its value, and to pay her subsidy to the end of the year. The sum was modest but it had to be found from somewhere, with, if possible, enough extra to form a small endowment for a theatre which still had only two reliably seat-filling dramatists, Lady Gregory and Boyle. Synge was potentially a money-maker, but they could not know this, since Nationalist boycotting was still causing his plays to be acted to half-empty houses.

As usual, the main weight of collecting subscriptions fell

on Lady Gregory, and as usual, she incurred the gibe that the
theatre was a Unionist tool because she turned to the people
who had money to give. Nevertheless, a year's respite was
something — and then in May it appeared that there was to
be no respite after all. Edward VII died, and the other Dublin
theatres closed.

Yeats was abroad, Lady Gregory at Coole, and the Abbey
was in charge of a new manager, Lennox Robinson, who was
scarcely more than a boy. 'God Save the King' had never
been sung at Abbey performances, and he did not see why
these should be interrupted for the monarch's demise, but as
a precaution he wired to Lady Gregory. She replied: 'Should
close through courtesy,' but her answer took three hours to
reach him, and the matinée had already begun. (It has been
suggested that the Gort telegraph-boy was a Nationalist, and
if he was still the Ferdy of *Hyacinth* this is quite probable.)
The harm being already done, Robinson continued with the
evening performance. Miss Horniman was furious. She
declared that the opening was not only disgraceful but
'political', demanded an apology from Lady Gregory and the
dismissal of Lennox Robinson, and not receiving what she
considered satisfaction on either count, announced her
withdrawal of the subsidy.

It was not so much the loss of the money that was serious,
as the damaging effect of Miss Horniman's trumpetings
among precisely those people to whom Lady Gregory was
turning for financial help. The Abbey was made to appear in
their eyes a nest of disloyalty and disaffection, and of course
Miss Horniman must have been perfectly aware of this. It is
hard to resist the suspicion that she was out to kill the theatre
if she could. One of her yellow-notepaper letters warns the
theatre staff in tones of barely disguised triumph that they
will all be out of work by Christmas.

But they were not. The Abbey was not a rich woman's

Irish toy, it was an idea in the minds of working dramatists, which had preceded her money and would outlive it. Lady Gregory rose to the challenge with renewed effort and courage, canvassing and campaigning. Yeats delivered a series of subscription lectures, and the Abbey's autumn season in London did well. By July of the following year, Blunt notes in his diary: 'Lady Gregory has been very successful this year with her plays, having cleared £500 by her theatrical visit to London and got £3000 of subscriptions.'

Her London base of operations was the historic house Hugh Lane had bought in Cheyne Walk, overlooking the Thames. His sister Ruth Shine, a beautiful young woman recently widowed, kept house for him, and with this nephew and niece her link was a particularly close and sympathetic one. The little yellow drawing-room at Lindsey House was made over to her as a sitting-room and theatrical office whenever she was in town; and in the evenings there were delightful and stimulating dinner-parties, for Lane was another of those who 'knew everybody'. She was introduced to a young man as 'the great Lady Gregory', and 'he seemed so excited I thought perhaps I really was great, but it was only because he had a friend who wants to get into the Abbey company'. Once the young people even forced her into fancy-dress and carried her off to a ball.

For all its anxieties, this was probably her finest hour, one which used her to capacity, both as organiser and as creator. And from it date what are probably the two best likenesses of her, certainly the two that best correspond to the mental picture formed by one who never saw her in the flesh.

She had a great distaste for being photographed, the result, no doubt, of her conviction that she was plain-looking, and few snapshots or news-pictures of her exist; I have been unable to find one of her and Yeats together, though they must have been a familiar couple on the Dublin scene. She

The Epstein bust. Reproduced by courtesy of the
Dublin Municipal Gallery of Modern Art.

had more faith in portraitists, but I do not know that it was altogether justified. The J. B. Yeats of 1903, which I reproduce, is charming in its eager girl-student look, but must surely flatter in terms of age; it is, rather, how she must have looked in her married years. The Mancini of 1906 in the Dublin Municipal Gallery was her own favourite, but it seems to me to give altogether too soft an impression of her personality; the later Orpen and Gerald Kelly portraits, on the other hand, are too glaring and harsh, the Orpen particularly seeming to have been painted with acute dislike.

But Lane made her sit to Epstein for a portrait bust, and this (also in the Municipal Gallery) is said by all who remember her to be an uncannily good likeness. She has described how the sculptor caught that vivid animation: 'one day some writer came in, asking questions about the work of our Theatre, and I was over-ready to answer and grew eager in talk and forgot the calmness that befits sculpture . . . and then I found that he had cut through the clay throat, tilting head and chin in an eternal eagerness.'

The other likeness is a photograph taken by Ruth Shine in the doorway of Lindsey House. For the beloved niece she did agree to pose, and the result has lain unseen for nearly fifty years in the photographer's album. This is Augusta Gregory's look, this haunting blend of authority and sombreness and humour, when she was at the height of her powers, when she wrote *Grania*.

3

Not since *Twenty-Five* had she shown any signs of abating her view that love was not a ruling passion in Ireland. Now, in *Grania*, she has an apparent change of heart, and writes a three-act play with only three characters, who have nothing to talk about but love. To Yeats, who expressed scepticism over the subject, she explained that 'the talk of lovers is inexhaustible, being of themselves and one another'.

The paring-down of the cast list, by which *The Poorhouse* gained so much when it was transformed into *The Workhouse Ward*, continued to exert her mind; she speaks wistfully of writing a play for one actor and a scarecrow. (She would certainly have appreciated Mr Samuel Beckett's *tour de force* for one actor and a tape-recorder.) Professor Ellis-Fermor, while admitting the fascination of *Grania*, thinks it a pity that so much was sacrificed to a technical fetish, and believes it would have gained from a complement of commentators, old nurses and suchlike confidantes. But here she has surely missed the point. *Grania* has only three characters because it is in a special sense a triangle drama, with which no outsider has anything to do.

Deirdre in the ancient legend is the good lover, who dies rather than give herself to the oppressor. Grania is the bad one, who comes finally to the tyrant's bed even though he has her true love's blood on his hands. This enigma challenged Lady Gregory, to whom the bad and adventurous women had always seemed so much more real than the good and acquiescent ones. 'The riddle she asks us through the ages is: Why did I, having left great grey-haired Finn for comely Diarmuid, turn back to Finn in the end, when he had consented to Diarmuid's death? And a question tempts one more than the beaten path of authorised history. If I have held but lightly to the legend, it is not because I do not know it, for in *Gods and Fighting Men* I have put together and rejected many versions.'

I should not have said myself that she holds to the legend 'but lightly'. All its salient features are in her play: Grania's virtual abduction of an unwilling Diarmuid, Diarmuid's promise to Finn that he will not sleep with her and will send an unbroken loaf each month as token of his faith, the seven years of enforced chastity, ending with an almost accidental breaking of the promise, Finn's revenge in sending Diarmuid to his death by trickery, Grania's *volte-face*, the jeers of Diarmuid's friends among the Fianna as she goes out to face them with Finn's crown on her head. What Lady Gregory has done is to simplify, to cut out the supernatural element, and to supply the essential clue.

The first act establishes Finn's tenderly paternal feeling for the young princess who comes to Almhuin as his bride, her innocence already troubled by love for a passing stranger. Diarmuid arrives, and proves to be the stranger, and Grania is undone. She begs him to flee with her; Finn overhears and is terrible in his wrath; she cannot return in disgrace to her father and has nowhere to go. Out of pity Diarmuid takes her beyond reach of Finn's vengeance, making first his vow of chastity.

When the second act opens, they have been wandering for seven years and are lovers at last. Their happiness appears idyllic, but it is flawed. Diarmuid took her because he found her in the arms of another man, the King of Foreign. They endlessly argue the incident — not in order that we, the audience, shall be informed of it, but because it is a sore point with both of them, there is something about it that is not 'right'. He is brooding and angry because the insult to his mistress is unavenged, she because she suspects that he came to her through jealousy and not through love. She begins to hanker for courts and cities and admiration, in order that he may still desire her. 'It is hard to nourish pride in a house having two in it only.'

At the height of their quarrel there comes a masked messenger from Finn, to know why he has not received his unbroken loaf. Grania breaks a loaf and bids him to take it back to his master with a taunting reply. The messenger, who seems to know a great deal about them, taunts Diarmuid in his turn, that the King of Foreign is living yet and goes boasting on his road. Diarmuid, thrusting aside Grania's desperate pleas, seizes his sword and rushes out to meet his enemy.

At the opening of the third act, Finn finds Grania anxious and alone. She returns his reproaches tenfold, heaping bitterness on him for the seven years of love and youth wasted. He tells her that he has sent Diarmuid to judgment, and she realises that the masked messenger was the King himself in disguise. Diarmuid is carried in dying. He regains consciousness for a few moments but fails to recognise his wife; all his love goes out to Finn. He remembers that they quarrelled, but cannot imagine why. Was it over a dog? 'Was not Hazel my own hound?'

Finn laments his favourite; henceforward he will have no more joy in anything; he tells Grania she is free. Then she rounds on him. She will go with him, Diarmuid is no more to her now than a sod that has been quenched with the rain. He believes at first that grief has unhinged her, but her mind is perfectly clear.

'He had no love for me at any time. It is easy know it now. I knew it all the while, but I would not give in to believe it. His desire was all the time with you yourself, and Almhuin. . . . Does any man at all speak lies at the very brink of death, or hold any secret in his heart? It was at that time he had done with deceit, and he showed where his thought was, and had no word at all for me that had left the whole world for his sake, and that went wearing out my youth, pushing here and there as far as the course of the stars of Heaven. . . . You are craving to get rid of me now, and to put me away out of your thoughts, the same as Diarmuid did. But I will not go! I will hold you to your word, I will take my revenge on him! He will think to keep your mind filled with himself and to keep me from you, he will be coming back showing himself as a ghost about Almhuin. He will think to come whispering to you, and you alone in the night time. But he will find me there before him! He will shrink away lonesome and baffled! I will have my turn that time. It is I will be between him and yourself, and will keep him out of that lodging for ever!'

Nothing the stricken Finn can say will move her. She snatches from him the crown that has been so many times offered to her, and sets it on her head. She opens the door, and faces the jeering of Diarmuid's warrior comrades. It stops suddenly as they see the terrible look on her face.

4

As I see it, *Grania* is not in the strict sense a love-story at all. It is a play in which a woman is ousted from an emotional relationship between two men. The 'love' is that of man for man, of brother for brother; it is loyalty to the warrior band, and a corresponding resentment of the woman who takes away the warrior's freedom, makes trouble with his comrades, distracts him from his purpose in life. It is an attitude which filters through the play as light filters through crystal; which runs through the heroic Irish sagas as it runs through the Greek. Its continuing validity was borne out by all Lady Gregory had observed in the world around her, the world of the 'loveless Irishman', the peasant society which relegated women to serfdom, the middle-class intellectual society which left them only the donkey-work.

For note that it is not Finn alone who robs Grania of Diarmuid. 'His desire was all the time with you yourself, and Almhuin.' Almhuin, the charmed circle of hunters and warriors; its modern equivalent was the masculine society of clubs and bars, of wit and talk and stimulus, from which a woman, through her talent as much a part of the movement as any of them, would be forever excluded. As an artist, needing to share, deserving to share, how could she fail to experience the frustrations that have been sublimated in the character of Grania?

And such a view of the Irishwoman's role, of her relegation to insignificance and her resentment under it, is not exclusively feminine. It is abundantly confirmed by Synge. His heroines,

Nora Burke, Sarah Casey, Pegeen Mike, are creatures caged and raging, given no scope for their powers, condemned to love men who are poor things beside them and do not really care for them at all. O'Casey's Juno offers further positive support,* and on the negative side, so to speak, are the quantities of second-rate Irish plays and stories that have for their mainspring a panic dislike of women, invariably represented as shrews, hussies and Aunt Sallies at whom anything can be thrown. A woman has only to put her nose into a saloon bar in any of the Celtic countries to realise that Almhuin is with us still.

Grania has not yet been professionally acted. The explanation given by Dr Lennox Robinson is that Lady Gregory could not find a cast to her liking. In 1911 Maire O'Neill, Synge's exquisite Pegeen, was at the zenith of her beauty, and the part of Grania was probably written with her in mind, but the right men were lacking. Maire O'Neill left to marry G. H. Mair in 1912, but the marriage was a failure and she returned to the Abbey at the end of 1916, a period when Lady Gregory's authority as director was very great. F. J. McCormick, whom many hold to have been the Abbey's finest heroic actor, joined the company a year or so later. There could therefore have been little difficulty about casting the play towards the end of the first war — admittedly a hard time for the Abbey, but other new plays were being put on. Yet to the best of Dr Robinson's recollection, *Grania* was never even brought forward as a possibility. Its creator seemed content to let it lie forgotten.

Did she 'take against' it, as she had against *Twenty-Five*, and if so, why? Did she doubt whether, after all, she could hold an audience's attention through three acts with only

---

* Synge and O'Casey have in common a genuine sympathy and liking for women, rare among Irish dramatists. May this be one reason why their pictures of human nature seem so much more solid and complete?

three persons? The doubt may be justified, but only the test of production could resolve it.

Or is it, perhaps, that the play tells one truth too many, and that when she came to think it over, she was disquieted by what she had done?

5

Only in one of her plays do I find the authentic note of physical passion between man and woman, and that is in the one-act tragedy of *MacDonough's Wife*, where the woman who inspires it is dead.

The figure of the wandering vernacular poet, 'in the succession of those who had made and recited their lyrics on the Irish roads before Chaucer wrote,' had always meant much to her. We have seen what she did to preserve Raftery's memory, and MacDonough has elements of Raftery, his confidence, his arrogant consciousness of descending from a mighty line of talent, the contemptuous courage with which he meets poverty and defeat. But the character is more directly drawn from the piper of the sheep-shearings at Roxborough, whom she could remember in his splendid youth, and whom she had watched grow into an old man. The story of his having no money for his wife's burial is, she says, based on reality.

Someone did her the honour of comparing this play with Synge's *Riders to the Sea*, but MacDonough is not a figure Synge would have drawn; he is altogether too heroic. Synge has no heroes, only heroines; his men are more harshly handled. What does lift the play almost to his level is a greater richness of language than she achieves elsewhere. Not merely does MacDonough speak like a poet; the two old women who are grudging guardians of his wife's body in the Galway lodging-house have a harsh folk-poetry in their sayings which contrasts with his wild imagery, as when one of them tells him that 'there is no one at all can put away from his road the bones and the thinness of death.'

When the play opens they are waiting for his return from the sheep-shearing at Cregroostha (Roxborough) and discussing the probable pauper burial of the dead woman, whom they have not liked. This resentment and suspicion of her felt by her neighbours is highly effective; we understand that she was 'a man's woman', that her passionate absorption in her husband was an outrage, almost an indecency, to the women of the herd. MacDonough's paroxysm of grief when he comes home and learns the news, the portrait he draws of her in his lamentation, complete the impression of a fierce, untamed spirit, who was loving only to him:

'I to bring you travelling, you were the best traveller and the best stepper, and the best that ever faced the western blast, and the waves of it blowing from you the shawl! I to be sore in the heart with walking you would make a smile of a laugh. I would not feel the road having your company; I would walk every whole step of Ireland. I to bring you to the dance-house you would dance till you had them all tired, the same in the late of the day as in the commencement! Your steps following quick on one another the same as hard rain on a flagstone! They could not find your equal in all Ireland or in the whole ring of Connemara!'

He rages at the thought of the workhouse burial. Well, then, say the old women, let him pay for decent mourners and bearers, he who must have earned fifty pounds from the quality at Cregroostha. He turns out his pockets and shows them empty. Where has the money gone? 'Thrown on counters, thrown on the drink-house floor, given for spirits, given for porter, thrown for drinks for friends and acquaintances, for strangers and strollers and vagabonds. Scattered in the parish of Ardrahan and at Labane cross. Tramps and schemers lying drunk and dead drunk at the butt of every wall.' The old women are openly triumphant at his self-reproach. It serves him right for marrying a strange wild girl, who was not liked in Galway.

Then his courage comes back to him.

'I am of the generation of Orpheus, and have in me the breed of his master, and of Raftery and Carolan and O'Daly and all that made sounds of music from this back to the foundations of the earth! And as to the rich of the world, I would not humble my head to them. Let them have their serving-men and their labourers and messengers will do their bidding. But the servant I myself command is the pipes that draws its breath from the four winds, and from a wind is beyond them again, and at the back of the winds of the air.'

He rushes into the street, and his pipes are heard in a piercing lament which brings the people flocking, clamouring for the honour of carrying his Catherine. He chooses whom he will have, 'no traffickers to put their shoulders under you, or any that made a refusal, or any seaside man at all.' He will have only the sheep-shearers from Cregroostha, who are in Galway for the fair. They enter in their cloaks of white flannel, and carry Catherine MacDonough away to the grave of a prince's bride.

MacDonough's Wife was written on board ship, when she was crossing the Atlantic to shepherd the Abbey company on their first American tour. Mr Brinsley Macnamara, who had gone with them as scene-shifter and office-boy, remembers her arriving with an illegible half-typed, half-scribbled manuscript, and how he helped her to make a fair copy. To my mind it is among the best half-dozen of her plays, and it forms a splendid coda to her tragedies, as *The Bogie Men* does to her comedies. The great chapter in her creative life is brought to a worthy close.

X

America

I

To take the Abbey to America had long been a dream with Yeats and Lady Gregory. Indeed, they were prepared for it to die there. If, she says, the subscription appeal had failed, 'we would take our reserve fund and spend it mainly on that voyage and that venture.' Happily, no such drastic step proved necessary. The company's fame had been spreading, and in the summer of 1911 they received an offer from Liebler, the American theatrical agents, to undertake a tour on generous terms. In Boston they were to open the new Liebler theatre, the Plymouth; in New York their theatre was to be the attractive Maxine Elliott. *The Playboy* was specially asked for. Liebler were not perturbed by the probability of Irish-American riots on the pattern of the Dublin Nationalist ones. They were cheerfully prepared to regard it as an advertisement.

Yeats sailed with the company, and supervised the Boston opening; Lady Gregory followed by the next boat. It was arranged between them that she would be in charge for the tour, while he returned home, but that she could summon him back if for any reason she found the responsibility too much.

She arrived in Boston on September 29th, and at once felt, as so many Irish do, that America was much less of a foreign country than England. Boston's reputation for standoffishness was certainly not endorsed by her; on the contrary, it seemed practically an extension of Galway, and many former

Roxborough and Coole tenants called upon her in their new glory of stylish clothes and visiting-cards. Indeed, all through the tour she was to have this pleasing experience, as Sir William had had fifty-two years before. She was amused and a trifle flattered by American interviewing methods and the amount of personal publicity she got, though piqued when one young woman with whom she had declined to discuss *The Playboy* wrote that 'my dress — Paris! — had no relation to the prevailing modes'. It had probably come from Paris a good many years before.

She was kept busy rehearsing *The Playboy*, because there was a new Pegeen, Eithne Magee, to be trained; but she saw as much as she could of the countryside, looking its most beautiful in the fall colourings, and soon had made a new friend. Mrs Jack Gardner was a wealthy widow who had devoted her fortune to the building of a 'Venetian' house and the amassing of an art-collection which were to be handed over to the people of Boston as a gift. She had obvious points of similarity with Enid Layard, and the same *grande dame* manner which Lady Gregory always wistfully admired.

But there was also a parallel with Hugh Lane, who had used a fortune made from dealing in Old Masters to buy the as yet unfashionable French Impressionists, and was proposing to make a gift of thirty-nine canvases to Dublin. The citizens of Boston had shown themselves very nearly as suspicious and unappreciative of Mrs Gardner's generosity as those of Dublin were proving over Hugh Lane's, and unlike Mrs Gardner, Lane could not afford to provide the art-gallery too. Dublin, he insisted, must build that, and Dublin was making every excuse to shelve the matter, and to cast aspersions on the pictures, so little resembling 'those beautiful productions displayed in the windows of our city picture shops.'

It was in the spacious music-room of Fenway Court that Lady Gregory made her debut as a public speaker. 'Saying a few words' at clubs and gatherings throughout the tour was a part of the manager's duties she had not bargained for, and the prospect dismayed her. Not only was she quite without experience, but her voice was soft and singsong ('whining', those who disliked her say), and she doubted if it would carry. She drafted a little lecture on the art of playwriting, and got to her feet, and her fears proved to have been groundless. 'It is a great relief to me and the discovery of a new faculty,' she wrote home. 'I shan't feel nervous again.'

Thereafter, her lecturing in margin of the tour took her to many places which the company did not visit. Her mind became a shifting panorama of sunlit impressions, as she looked in on kindly cities, 'where strangers welcomed me and I seemed to say goodbye to friends. Dozing in midnight trains, I would remember, as in a dream, "the flight of a bird through a lighted hall", the old parable of human life.'

She was enchanted by the college-girl audiences at Vassar and Smith, their fearlessness and freedom from convention. At Vassar there was a football team, 'all dressed as boys, had made-up trousers, or knickers, and some were playing on combs to represent a band.' The President, one of the few men in her audience of six hundred there, sat near the door and promised to hold up his handkerchief if he could not hear her properly. Half-way through he raised it slowly and she stopped, disconcerted; but the poor man only wanted very badly to blow his nose. Her plays were known and loved in both colleges, and the Smith girls had conjugated a new verb, 'to Jackdaw'.

Yeats stayed to see through the first night of *The Playboy* in Boston on October 16th, but in spite of a good many attacks in the papers beforehand, it went off peaceably, partly because the audience was well laced with Harvard boys determined it should be heard. The Mayor set his seal of approval on the plays and there was no further trouble.

At Providence, the first place to be visited after Boston, a complaint had been made to the police commissioners, but she appeared before them and answered all the objections raised, and the commissioners themselves then attended a performance of *The Playboy* and declared that they had enjoyed every minute of it. Lowell, New Haven, Albany and Washington were visited triumphantly; at Washington she was invited to the White House and presented to President Taft, and she took the players on a picnic to Mount Vernon, and told them how her grandfather had been a friend of George Washington, and had given the name of Mount Vernon to his sea-lodge on the Burren coast.*

But newspaper growlings against *The Playboy* had been following them round, and were mounting in New York ahead of them. New York was to be the showdown, and a grateful sight when she arrived there on November 18th was her old friend John Quinn, the brilliant lawyer who had been a supporter of the Irish Renascence before the Abbey was even a name.

2

She was delighted with the Maxine Elliott Theatre. The only thing lacking in it, as in most American theatres, was a green-room, on which a 'family' company like the Abbey so much depended for its corporate feeling. But she was allotted a little sitting-room off the stage, which had been Maxine Elliott's own, and there she re-started her tea-parties for players and wellwishers, doubtless with the nearest equivalent to a barmbrack that the New York bakers could produce.

* There has been some confusion over the family properties on the Burren coast. Mount Vernon, a most attractive and by no means small Regency house, had passed out of Persse ownership, no doubt in one of the family's financial crises, before Lady Gregory's time, and was replaced as a holiday home by Chevy Chase. It became Gregory property for a while after Robert Gregory's marriage, when he bought it as a seaside house for his children. It was at no time, any more than Coole was, the personal property of Lady Gregory.

The wellwishers were numerous and encouraging, but there were also a good many Job's comforters, who brought in horrific stories of the savagery being organised for the first night of *The Playboy*, and of preaching by Catholic priests against all the plays. It was only, of course, a section of the New York priesthood, and a leading Catholic hostess gave a lunch-party in her honour in order to show that intelligent Catholic opinion was on her side.

The Playboy was not due till the second week, which meant a hiatus trying to the nerves. The repertoire of the first week was excellently received, and the first night was something of a Gregory triumph, since it consisted of two of her plays, *Spreading the News* and *Rising*, together with T. C. Murray's *Birthright*. Maire nic Shiubhlaigh, who had overcome her dislike of receiving a salary sufficiently to rejoin the company, but not her resentment at the ascendancy of director over players, grudgingly admits that *Rising* 'went over with almost startling success'.

At the weekend, Lady Gregory visited the Theodore Roosevelts, who were old friends. The ex-President was still a person of incomparable influence, and she asked him to lend the *Playboy* first night his support, but his wife was not well, and he felt himself unable to leave home.

November 27th dawned ominously, with a leader in the *Gaelic-American* predicting that 'the New York Irish will send the Anti-Irish Players back to Dublin like whipped curs'. Quinn warned her of definite demonstrations being prepared. So much the better, she said; let the enemy show themselves, they had been threatening too long. She agreed to have the theatre policed, however, since they were now in a country where the police were not regarded as agents of an occupying power.

The Gaol Gate was the curtain-raiser, and it was given before a packed but restless house. The editor of the *Gaelic-*

American and his bodyguard were pointed out to her in two
rows of the stalls, and other disturbers were strategically
placed in little groups. They went into action soon after
Playboy began, Christy's confession of having murdered his
father being the signal. It was the Dublin second night over
again: boos and shouts, showers of rotten vegetables, and an
odious refinement, cubes filled with assafoetida, which burst
as they hit the stage.

'I went round when the disturbance began,' she says, 'and
knelt in the opening of the hearth, calling to every actor who
came within earshot that they must not stop for a moment
but must spare their voices, as they could not be heard, and
we should do the whole act over again.' Maire nic Shiubhlaigh
remembers her as 'rotund, thin-lipped and very determined-
looking', shouting 'Keep playing!" Finally the house lights
went on, the curtain came down and the audience gave itself
up to a free fight. The police were given the order to arrest
the obvious trouble-makers, and Fred O'Donovan, the
Christy, appealed from the stage for another hearing. The
last mutterings from the gallery were drowned by cries of
admiration from the stalls, and on the littered and filthy stage
the play began again. It was not heard precisely in silence, but
at any rate it was heard. The mob had not, as in Dublin, won.

Ten men were arrested and fined, and an impressive
collection of spoils, 'chiefly stink-pots and rosaries', was
displayed in the box office next morning.

The second night was distinguished, and calmed, by the
presence of Theodore Roosevelt, who was not willing to
have his friend and the work of Synge again insulted. He
found time to dine with Lady Gregory and share her box
next to the stage; the audience rose and cheered him as he
entered it, and he firmly handed his hostess forward to take
the applause. This took the heart out of the opposition, who
raised their voices from time to time but were quickly snubbed

by those around them. Roosevelt went backstage after the first act, was introduced to the company, and told them, using her own phrase, that they were increasing the dignity of Ireland. At the end of the performance he gave her his arm, and 'we found the whole route to the door packed, just a narrow lane we could walk through, and everyone taking off hats and looking at him with real reverence and affection, so unlike those royal crowds in London.* It was an extraordinary kindness that he did us.'

After that there was no real fight left in the New York Irish, and the publicity they had given the Abbey ensured packed houses and extended the tour to the beginning of March. 'I was afraid more people had come to see us pelted than playing,' Lady Gregory confessed to a luncheon audience. But in fact American appreciation of the plays, her own no less than Synge's, was wholehearted. Sometimes the two of them became a trifle confused in the audience's mind. She was asked 'what was her moral purpose in writing *The Playboy*', and someone was overheard debating the merits of 'Lady Gregory's play *The Cowboy of the Western World*'.

New York was the worst hurdle, but they were mistaken if they imagined there were to be no others. Philadelphia and Chicago had interesting variations in store.

3

The Playboy was held back till the second week in Philadelphia, as it had been in New York. Its first night began noisily, and for about ten minutes the players could not be

---

* Though she admired the Empress Frederick, who was a friend of Lady Layard's, she had little use for any other members of the Royal Family, who seem to have epitomised English Philistinism in her eyes. One of the most amusing passages in Blunt's diaries describes her mimicking the German accents and court banalities of 'two little maids of all work' who had called unexpectedly on Lady Layard in Venice, and proved to be Queen Alexandra and the Empress of Russia.

heard, but this time she declined to make them repeat it.
'I thought the audience ought to be made to suffer for not
being more helpful.' The police were called in and ejected a
good many people, and by the second night she had organised
her own strong-arm squad, having lectured at the University
and invited eight of its leading athletes to be her guests at the
play. Their presence proved more effective than that of the
Trinity students had been, and Philadelphia appeared
conquered.

However, under a local law any citizen had the right to
bring a charge of indecency against theatrical companies
appearing within its boundaries, and this manoeuvre was
next tried. Lady Gregory was warned that if she did not
withdraw *The Playboy* pending an enquiry, she and the whole
cast would be technically liable to arrest. She at once telephoned to their legal champion, Quinn, and told him that
'I would sooner go to my death than give in', adding charac-
teristically: 'I should like to avoid arrest, because of the
publicity; one would feel like a suffragette.'

By the time Quinn could arrive from New York, the
'technical arrest' had been made, and as it was a process not
very well understood in England or Ireland, the newspaper
headlines gave Yeats and the Abbey's London friends a
considerable jar. In fact, the manager of the theatre went bail
for the appearance of the company before the magistrates
later in the week, and *The Playboy* continued before record
audiences.

There was a farcical appearance in the magistrates' court,
followed by an even more Gilbertian trial before a judge, at
which Quinn made mincemeat of witnesses whose knowledge of the play was as sketchy as their critical approach was
naïve. One of them claimed that there was immorality in the
fact of Christy and Pegeen being left alone in the house at
night. Had immorality taken place on the stage? — Quinn

asked. Well, no, admitted the witness, but they all knew what
happened when the curtain fell.

There was no real case against the Abbey players, but to
their disappointment, the judge felt himself unable to make a
decision on the spot. They left Philadelphia still under bail and
the imputation of putting on indecent plays. They could not
be prevented from continuing their tour, and when they
reached Pittsburgh, the last stop but one before Chicago,
Lady Gregory was able to announce to the evening audience
that the case against the company had been dismissed. But
there was a new crop of rumours that trouble on the grand
scale was being stirred up in Chicago. 'I feel like Wilhelm
Meister,' she wrote home, 'going through ever-fresh adventures with the little troop.'

Chicago was under snow, and an 'Anti-Irish Players'
League' had been formed, with an initial membership of
three hundred. 'Such a pity I couldn't have slipped in to the
meeting!' she commented. Petitions had been circulated and
were said to have been signed by thousands. The players were
news, and once again she was surrounded by reporters. They
were mostly young boys who with very little encouragement
were telling her the story of their lives and bringing out
snapshots of their fiancées, and in no time she had them
running about helpfully, just as she had the Philadelphia
students.

There were continual false alarms that the Mayor had
yielded to pressure and banned *The Playboy*. Finally His
Honour announced that he had 'read part of it and its chief
characteristic seems to be stupidity rather than immorality'.
The play opened on February 8th, so peaceably that, she says,
she nearly fell asleep. Chicago's bark was worse than its bite.
In fact, virtually the only bite it offered was an anonymous
letter to Lady Gregory herself. 'This is to console you from
the dread that may fill your grizzly heart after you have read

the contents of this note *your fate is sealed* never again shall you gase on the barren hilltops of Connemara. . . .' It was ornamented with drawings of a coffin and a pistol, and was not a document to intimidate the sister of the dead-shot Persses, for, she says, she did not think from the drawing that the sender had much practical knowledge of firearms. She continued to walk unprotected every night from the La Salle Hotel to the theatre.

The company returned home in March, to be greeted with a gala public reception at the Royal Hibernian Academy. It was a triumph for the players, who had stood up so gallantly to trial by stink-bomb and war of nerves,but above all it was a triumph for Lady Gregory as their leader. Hard fact, however, was not allowed to cramp the style of the fanatics on the Nationalist side, and they continued to spread their statements that *The Playboy* was 'dead as a doornail' and 'had been hissed from the stage in New York'. It was to combat these lies that she sat herself down to write her personal history of the Abbey Theatre, culminating in a long chapter on the American adventure, while it was still fresh in her mind.

4

Though her best work as a creator had been completed before she set foot in Boston, as an organiser Lady Gregory reached in this first American tour the summit of her powers. Hitherto she had been Yeats's second-in-command; even in the Dublin *Playboy* battle, she had only stood alone for a couple of nights, before he arrived to take control. But on the strenuous and nerve-racking American road the leadership was hers unshared. The knowledge that she could summon him in an emergency must have been reassuring, but in fact she met nothing that her ability and courage were unequal to.

The consequent gain in her self-confidence was great.

Indeed, there would be plenty in anti-feminist Dublin to accuse her of having too much; but it was certainly a quality she was going to need in the difficult years immediately ahead.

And the happiest aspect of the tour for her was that it had made money — real money, not the few hundreds of a London season, or the pathetic head-above-water budget of the last years in Dublin. She on whom the brunt of the begging had fallen, and who alone seriously worried about the miserable salaries paid to the players, had now proved that the Abbey need no longer be an object of patronage by the rich. It could pay its own way. Its friends in London and across the Atlantic could make it independent of neglectful Dublin, and lay the acid interfering ghost of Miss Horniman for ever.

At the end of the year, she and the troop set out again, and this time Montreal was included in their tour. 'There were no riots,' she says, 'and we were of the happy people who have no history.' Lennox Robinson recollects disturbances here and there, but the stuffing had gone out of the opposition. She was now greatly preoccupied with the affairs of Hugh Lane and his pictures. Relations between him and the Dublin Corporation had steadily worsened, they were objecting to the Lutyens plan for a gallery on which he had set his heart, and he was threatening to remove the pictures from Dublin altogether and lend them to the National Gallery in London.

She spoke of her anxieties to her old friends the reporters of Chicago, and the resultant publicity showed that there would be generous American response to an appeal. Accordingly the company gave a matinée towards the gallery fund and raised £200, and a group of business men guaranteed £1000, a gesture which was repeated when the tour proceeded to Philadelphia and Montreal. Boston and Mrs Gardner were welcoming and open-handed as ever, and Lane wrote: 'If the pictures are saved for Dublin it is entirely owing to you and the generosity of your American friends.'

But it was all wasted effort, for Dublin Corporation refused to let a Lutyens gallery straddle the Liffey, (in which decision, at least, they were surely right,) and Lane was by now so exacerbated by their obvious lack of enthusiasm for his gift that in the autumn he removed it, sent it to London, and made his fatal new will. His aunt went sadly back to her tree-planting at Coole.

Nor was America to prove, after all, a permanent solution of the Abbey's financial troubles. This second tour made money, though not so much as the first. The third showed a small loss.

Conditions were against it. The company sailed in December of 1914, and though America had not yet entered the war, its shadow darkened all artistic enterprise. Lady Gregory, however, blamed the failure on Lennox Robinson, the company's manager, for 'running from place to place' and visiting too many small towns. Robinson resigned on their return, and so the Abbey lost its most consistently successful manager and producer during the years when its survival was most critical.

'I expect I did muddle things,' said Dr Robinson with an infinitely rueful grace when, from what was all too evidently his deathbed, he answered my questions about Lady Gregory. He forbore to remind me, as he might well have done, that he was still a very young man at that time and ought not to have been given so much responsibility. And it was unlike Lady Gregory to be hard on youth; in fact, I have not been told of any parallel instance. But in this case it is understandable. She had banked on finding financial emancipation in America, and the disappointment was correspondingly severe.

Happily, their differences were patched in the end. Lennox

Robinson returned in 1919, and from then on he and she were, as Mr Gerard Fay has acknowledged, the combination which pulled the Abbey through all its troubles. She would always keep a sharp and slightly severe eye on him, but I think his friends as well as hers will admit that it was what he needed. They were a team in the sense that each of them had what the other lacked.

If one were to draw a graph of her life, the curve would go downwards from the start of the third American tour. Hitherto, nothing had been made easy for her — far from it — but her career had been a steady series of faculties discovered, difficulties surmounted, battles won. Now, as her creative faculties lessened (a process which must always sadden the creator, no matter how clearly or sensibly it has been foreseen), so the world around her darkened grimly, and the Abbey's position became ever more precarious. Two dreadful personal losses stood ahead, and beyond that, the horror of a beloved country plunged into civil war.

The best was over, the worst was yet to come. But that is true of all our lives, and fortunately none of us can detect the watershed while we are in process of living them. In the case of Lady Gregory, a biographer cannot wish it otherwise. There is in her a resilience of spirit which makes it a pleasure to continue in her company, through the bad times as through the good.

XI

Historian and Biographer

———————

I

Conceive that a practising playwright, colleague of Molière and Racine, had written a book which took us behind the scenes and showed us their genius at work; would it not be required reading in every French lycée, would not whole passages of it be got by heart by every well-educated French child? And if a contemporary had performed a similar office for Shakespeare and Ben Jonson, it is likely that even the British educational authorities would get out a (possibly expurgated) school text. But Lady Gregory's *Our Irish Theatre*, which does precisely this for the Irish dramatic revival, is so thoroughly out of print that the only text available to me for a year was the solitary copy in the invaluable London Library, after which I could count myself lucky to pick up a copy in Dublin at a stiffish price.

'It is impossible not to think that the Establishment silently disapproves of the Irish Renascence,' writes a leading member of the Dublin book trade to whom I commented on this extraordinary neglect. 'Having read the syllabuses and looked over the prescribed textbooks it is apparent that there is nothing to distinguish the English course taught in Irish schools from that in any other English-speaking country. Both our universities for their B.A. pass course devote a term to Anglo-Irish literature but do not give it any special prominence.' In my own circle, the only acquaintance who had read *Our Irish Theatre* was a Frenchwoman who took her degree in English at the Sorbonne, thirty years ago. It certainly looks as though Synge is not the only native genius the Irish prefer to hush up.

If *Our Irish Theatre* were a dreary or badly-written book, it would still be immensely valuable; but it is nothing of the kind. It is hurriedly-written, and for this reason both Dr Lennox Robinson and Lady Gregory herself were hard on it, but there is gain as well as loss from speed of writing. The bubbling enthusiasm and raciness of the narrative make it intensely readable. Out she pours the adventures, aspirations, setbacks of the little group of friends, their lendings and borrowings, scraps from their letters, thumb-nail sketches of their characters; and we experience, what is so rare in books by writers about writing, something of the happiness as well as the effort and anxiety of literary creation.

Of course she is not setting out to write a textbook, or a dispassionate critical estimate. She is not an academic literary historian, but a creator, one of themselves, telling us how it is done. The best academic mind to have so far applied itself to the Irish Renascence, Professor Ellis-Fermor's, has made full use of the book and repeatedly acknowledged its value as taking us into 'the workshop of genius'.

And of course it is personal and discursive; it was impossible for her to write in any other way. But hers is the naturally sympathetic personality of the dramatist, which enhances, instead of obscuring, the characters she describes. Synge in *Our Irish Theatre* is not less himself because he is seen through her eyes; because she is visiting him in hospital and telling him of her search for Irish terrier puppies, and of the little house with a view to the hills where at last she found them, and because she remembers how he said wistfully that that was just the sort of Dublin home he longed for, and how they decided together that they felt 'more and more the time wasted that was not spent in Ireland'.

And if she is discursive, it is always, as one may say, to the point. At first sight there might seem something irrelevant in a lengthy portrait of Sir Frederick Burton, director of the National Gallery in London, Unionist and friend of Sir William, followed by an equally detailed portrait of John O'Leary, the Fenian leader and martyr, in his old age. But she has her purpose. She is showing us how widely rooted were the sympathies that nourished the infant theatre, from the Conservative Anglo-Irish gentleman to the working-class rebel. Similarly, the snippets of family history dotted through the book are never mere egotistical chitchat about Persses and Gregorys, but help to relate the literary movement to happenings of the immediate past.

Naturally, there is a good deal that she cannot say. Her account of Miss Horniman's part, for instance, is brief, though generous and graceful; in later years she was to regret that it had not been possible to show 'Miss Horniman on the warpath', but it was not within a lady's code to betray her disagreements with a benefactress. She criticises no one, not Martyn, nor the Fays, nor any of the others who swarmed off from the hive; they simply disappear from the text, in the case of the Fays with a little sigh of genuine regret: 'I am very sorry that they, who more almost than any others had laid the foundation of the Irish Theatre, did not wait with us for its success.' The only real villains of the piece, such as the Dublin Castle official who tried to bully her over *Blanco Posnet*, remain anonymous. When one considers the amount of personal polemics which has been brought into virtually every other autobiographical book by an Irish writer, Lady Gregory's restraint and good feeling appear very nearly miraculous.

For myself, I find *Our Irish Theatre* an enchanting as well as a deeply informative work, and I would not willingly lose a word of it, unless, perhaps, the apostrophes to her four-year-

M

old grandson, which now read a trifle coyly. What it does need, and was obviously due to receive from her, is correction and expansion. She speaks several times in the *Journals* of a projected History of the Abbey, which would presumably have incorporated this book and carried it further; and in a letter of 1927 to her great-nephew Desmond Shawe-Taylor she says: 'I wish I had the energy to re-write my book *Our Irish Theatre*, for it was hastily put together as a reply to endless questions. . . .'

Why, then, did she never do it? She still had 'energy' for revision and correction, but she devoted it to the typing — and here and there, it would seem, to the re-writing — of her *Journals*, which as far as her literary activities are concerned only begin in 1919, when most of her important work and all the Abbey's birth-pangs were over. One can only regret that her activity was not switched into fertile channels, instead of being allowed to stagnate in a pool of mainly family affairs.

The task remains for someone else; and if the Irish 'Establishment' are not to deserve the imputation cast on them by my friend of the Dublin bookshop, then they should finance some scholar to do the work properly, and re-issue it in an edition which every reader of Yeats and Synge can afford. It is mainly a question of filling in Lady Gregory's gaps and continuing the story beyond 1914. There are a few obvious misprints to correct, such as Miss Horniman's 'former' letter on page 39, where the text plainly requires 'formal'; and the odd dates, notably that key starting-point of 1898, which should be a year earlier.

But Lady Gregory's general standards of honesty and accuracy are so high that the occasional slip can be forgiven her; she at least tries, whereas Yeats, with a similar temperamental allergy to 'dates and figures and the numbers of friends' houses in a street', gets over the problem by never, in his autobiographical writings, mentioning any dates at all.

2

The two plays she wrote in 1914, *Shanwalla* and *The Wrens*, differ greatly in calibre. Dr Robinson finds the three-act *Shanwalla* 'a strange, moving play, out of her vein and stupidly neglected'; but I find it inescapably one of her failures. The theme, of a young wife's return from the dead to defend her man falsely accused of murder, could have been moving, had it been handled by a dramatist who believed in the supernatural — not literally, of course, but imaginatively. Lady Gregory probably knew more ghost-stories than anyone in Ireland, but she knew them as collector and folklorist, not as a half-believer like Yeats. She remains the woman who could wander night and day in Coole's haunted woods and 'never see anything worse than herself'.

The Wrens on the other hand, a one-acter which is her last fling at folk-history, really has been 'stupidly neglected', to a point where it seems even to have disappeared from the list of Abbey first nights. Its story is of that nail for want of which the battle was lost. In the Irish version of the parable, the nail becomes the wrens who by pecking at the sentries' drums gave the alarm before the Battle of Clontarf.

The year is 1799, and the scene is laid outside the Dublin Parliament; within, members are debating the fatal Bill for union with England by which they will vote themselves out of existence. Lord Castlereagh's servant is contemptuously confident that the Bill will go through; Kirwan's is listening for the division bell, when he will summon his master to vote against it.

The 'wrens' come in, William and Margy Hevenor, strolling singers, penniless and quarrelling. He is a shiftless drunkard, she a young woman with possibilities of intelligence and self-respect, and a notion in her untutored mind that the passing of the Bill would be a shame and disgrace — 'It is England will get the cream and leave us the broken milk.' But her real longing is for security, a home for herself and their child, symbolised by the stuffed pincushion her husband has pawned for drink. 'My pincushion that I got from the minister's wife, and I a child rising up. The first little stick of furniture ever I had, and I bringing it from road to road till such time as I'd get a little table to put it on, and a room would hold the table, and the bed; and a little kitchen along with it, the way I'd be in Heaven having a little place of my own.'

The two lordly lackeys are amused by the pair, and Kirwan's servant suggests that the drunkard Hevenor shall take the pledge 'till the Union Bill will be thrown out, and that will be inside of a few hours'. That's no use, says Margy, where-upon her husband takes the pledge to spite her. Now, Castlereagh's servant is quick to point out, she has everything to gain by the Bill's going through; if it does, her man will have to stay sober for the rest of his life. And at once, alas, she changes sides.

Kirwan's servant denounces her perfidy, but she has an unanswerable feminine reply: 'It is not Ireland I have in charge. It is William Hevenor I have in charge. . . . If you had a hundred in family a husband is the nearest. Isn't it better to me Parliament to go to wrack in the clouds than my man to live blazing drunk?'

In his preoccupation with the argument, Kirwan's servant has failed to hear the division bell. Now comes news that the Bill has gone through — by one vote. For want of his master's vote, the Irish Parliament is lost.

It would have been tempting to end on a note of senti-mental heroics, with Margy repentant at having betrayed her country for a stuffed pincushion. But Lady Gregory knows her sex too well. Kirwan's servant is stricken, but Margy is triumphant. She tucks her unwillingly reformed drunkard under her arm, and goes off blithely to get the pincushion out of pawn. The symbolic overtones are there right enough, but they derive from a recognisable human melody, bravely sung.

3

The war years were even more nerve-racking for Lady Gregory than for the general run of mothers, for Robert Gregory had early transferred from the Connaught Rangers into the Royal Flying Corps, where life was notoriously short. Night and day she was haunted by the casualty lists, and the knowledge that the German machines were so much in advance of ours.

Then in May of 1915, she lost the other young man most dear to her. Hugh Lane, returning from a picture-dealing trip to the United States, sailed on the *Lusitania* and perished almost within sight of his Irish birthplace.

Relations between him and Dublin had greatly improved on his accepting (while refusing the salary) the directorship of the National Gallery of Ireland. At the same time he had fallen out of love with the London National Gallery, which had treated his gift quite as cavalierly as Dublin, and consigned most of his pictures — including, incredible as it may seem, the Renoir 'Parapluies' — to the cellars. She felt certain that he must have changed his mind and his will, and restored the pictures to his native country.

No document was to be found at Lindsey House, but she remembered the director's desk in the National Gallery of Ireland, and asked Ruth Shine to have it searched. And there, in a sealed envelope, was a codicil to his will, 'to the effect that the group of pictures now at the London National Gallery which I had bequeathed to that institution, I now bequeath to the City of Dublin, providing that a suitable

building is provided for them within 5 years of my death.'
The sole trustee, appointed to carry out the codicil, was his
aunt, Lady Gregory.

The document was signed or initialled in three places, but
he had forgotten to have it witnessed. In effect, therefore, he
had bequeathed to his aunt merely a burden and a frustration,
which were to endure to her life's end.

But for the time being she was not to realise this. She
rejoiced at the forgiving spirit shown by the codicil, and felt
confident that so unmistakable a proof of the testator's wishes
could ultimately be legalised. There was Ruth Shine to
testify that her brother had no business habits in the ordinary
way, and had had to be reminded by herself of the need to
get the original will witnessed; it was quite in keeping that
he should fail to realise that a codicil required a similar
formality. And there were a good many precedents for the
legalising of invalid wills where the testator's intentions were
not in doubt; while a Bill had already gone through Parliament to legalise the unwitnessed wills of soldiers who died on
active service.

It would all take time, and the middle of the war was not a
propitious moment for getting legislation started; but the
support reaching her from men of goodwill everywhere,
English no less than Irish, led her to suppose that when the
matter ultimately came up it would be plain sailing. But
Bernard Shaw struck an ominously prophetic note, when he
reminded her of the country saying that it is hard to get
butter out of a dog's mouth.

Meanwhile, the Abbey's affairs were preoccupation enough.
The war had thinned audiences cruelly: 'The Abbey is hard
hit but hopes to survive,' Yeats wrote to a friend in September
of 1915. The Easter Rising of the following year, when most
of the players downed greasepaint and put on rebel uniform,
did not help matters. She could never bring herself to condone

physical violence, not even in the Nationalist cause, but the brutality of the reprisals exacted confirmed her hatred of English rule.

This period of doldrums was also the period of constantly-replaced producers, for which also the blame has been laid at her door. The insinuation is that 'Lady Gregory was difficult to get on with', but a very little conversation with survivors of that time suggests that it was the company as a whole that was 'difficult to get on with', as, indeed, it always had been. It was still a band of individualists, working out of a sense of vocation and for wretchedly small pay, still as resentful of 'foreign' domination as when it had refused to accept Iden Payne over the head of Willie Fay. At least one of the producers was a distinguished dramatist, but to the players he was an Ulsterman, and they tittered at the Kensingtonian accents in which, it was alleged, his wife acted the heroines of Synge.

In January of 1918, the blow so long expected fell. Robert Gregory, whose survival till then had been something of a miracle, was shot down when returning from a successful flight over the Austrian lines in Italy. The disaster drew from Yeats three great elegies, which for nobility of language can stand beside *Lycidas* and *Adonais*, and give a far more immediate sense of personal loss. The picture that emerges from them of the mother, calm and self-forgetting in her sorrow, is confirmed by her letters answering the condolences of friends. They speak only of his qualities, and of the grief of her daughter-in-law and the uncertain future of her orphaned grandchildren, never of herself. She was, and she knew it, fortunate in still having important work to fill her life, and the habit of discipline to carry her forward, even though the emotional mainspring might be broken.

There is only one reference to the tragedy in the work published in her lifetime, and it ends the important autobiographical introduction to *The Kiltartan Poetry Book*. The poems are her translations of Irish folk-verse, and 'when in the first month of the new year I began to choose from among them, it seemed strange to me that the laments so far outnumbered any songs of joy. But before that month was out, news was brought to me that made the keening of women for the brave and for those who are left lonely after the young seem to be but the natural outcome and expression of human life.'

4

Yet it was in the war years that she found a new vein of sunny fantasy in the writing of fairy plays, 'I think perhaps through some unseen inevitable kick of the swing towards gay-coloured comedy from the shadow of tragedy.' The first two, *The Golden Apple* (1916) and *The Dragon* (1917) are the best, though they all have a charm and competence which put them far ahead of the average children's play, and an undercurrent of social satire which will keep the adult part of the audience amused.

It was not her first writing for children. *The Kiltartan History Book* had been published in 1909 with illustrations by Robert Gregory, *The Kiltartan Wonder Book* in 1910 with illustrations by his wife. Both are in fact straight folklore, told as if from the mouth of the grandfather gathering his children round the hearth, or of old Mary Sheridan at Roxborough. Lady Gregory may have shortened and simplified a little, but there is no attempt to 'write down' for children, and for this reason the books have a timeless quality which might well set them among the children's classics. Certainly, they deserve reprinting.

The notion of using folklore for a children's play had been in her mind for a long time before she wrote *The Golden Apple*, and as there was no possibility of putting on a spectacular piece under wartime stringency, she could think of it as something to be read rather than acted, and dovetail three or four stories together. (Presumably it was drastically cut when the Abbey finally produced it in 1920.) Murray brought it out in book form, again with enchanting and apposite illustrations by Margaret Gregory. The principal story is of the rescuing of a maiden in distress, and it gave Barry Fitzgerald a fine comic chance as Simon, the hero's Sancho Panza: 'I don't wish to be killed, where I was not brought up to it like kings' sons.' Among the embellishments is a giant who is really a fake on stilts and under the thumb of his wife.

The Dragon is even more amusing and much more coherent. The monster of the title demands a Princess as sacrifice, and the most unlikely people find courage to defend her. 'Change of heart' is how Lady Gregory herself saw, and originally titled, the play. 'All change more or less except the Queen. She is satisfied that she has moved all things well, and so she must remain till some new breaking-up or re-birth.' The Queen is a triumphant metamorphosis of the fairytale Wicked Stepmother, fussy, snobbish and interfering. She had been a governess before her elevation to the throne, and is full of pronouncements about 'how things were done at the King of Alban's court'.

Of the later fairy plays, *Aristotle's Bellows* leans rather too heavily on folk-song; it is almost a ballad opera. *The Jester* must be awkward to produce professionally, because the cast consists mainly of small boys, but it would make an attractive school play, and it embodies Lady Gregory's notion of how boys should be brought up. (A compromise, one may say, between the happy hedonism of Roxborough and the classical learning of Coole.)

When war ended and after Lennox Robinson had returned, the first three plays were put on at the Abbey with considerable success. Being laid in no particular time or place, they proved less difficult to dress and mount than had been feared. 'The Abbey rag-bag', as Yeats called the wardrobe department, made over some of the dresses Charles Ricketts had designed for his poetic plays, and unearthed a hamper of Elizabethan costumes presented years before by an English actress, and stage carpenter Sean Barlow's Dragon was a mechanical marvel almost up to Wagnerian standards. Among the most appreciative spectators were Douglas Hyde and his little daughter Nuala, who had given her name to the Princess in the play, while James Stephens and his children, the author notes proudly in her diary, 'shouted with delight'.

Leading parts in the fairy plays were created by Maureen Delany, who was only eclipsed by the Allgood sisters in Lady Gregory's estimation of actresses. Miss Delany, whose death while this edition was being prepared is a sad loss to stage and screen, came to the Abbey through the acting school that had been started while the company was in America. Her recollections of Lady Gregory have a warmth of humour and affection which are in refreshing contrast to the cold-shouldering of the Dublin literary world.

The directors watched progress in the acting school closely, and when Lady Gregory murmured to a student in her rather shy way, 'I think I have a little part for you', it was almost the equivalent of a gold medal at the R.A.D.A. Maureen Delany was soon promoted to the Sara Allgood parts in the Gregory one-acters, which, unlike their original creator, she played with the true Galway accent. But like the previous generation of pretty young girls, she sometimes caught herself wishing that Lady Gregory had written feminine leads nearer her own age, particularly as there was still no money to replace the terrible grey wigs, which felt like leaden helmets on one's head. Still, she relished the fun of the acting parts, especially Mrs Broderick in *The Jackdaw*.

Although Lennox Robinson was nominally the producer, he deferred to Lady Gregory in the final rehearsals of any new play by her, and a quaint contrast they made, he so abnormally tall and thin and she so tiny and rotund. She had clear ideas of what she wanted, and individual interpretation by the player was not encouraged beyond a certain point. (It was still a dramatist's theatre, not an actor's.) She worked her cast hard, but always with consideration. 'At first I had an ugly mannerism of bobbing my head forward,' Miss Delany recalled, 'and Lady Gregory cured me of it by making me rehearse with a book on my head.' She was probably not the only player to whom this Spartan method was applied.

Miss Delany was not of those who turned up their noses at the barmbrack; on the contrary, she found it very sustaining during the long hours of rehearsal. One reason why they were so long was that the Abbey still relied on amateurs to help out in small parts, and these could only come after their day's work was finished. Lady Gregory made allowances, but one was not expected openly to flag. Once, Miss Delany admitted, she was caught smothering a yawn. She was told with some severity: 'My dear, the audience may yawn if it likes, but never, never you!'

Lady Gregory was always accessible to the humblest member of the company, and so, for that matter, was Yeats, however Olympian he might seem to the outside world. They would always see you in the office, usually about a rise, and if they could possibly screw an extra five shillings a week out of the theatre's meagre finances, they would. This was one of the things about which producers complained — that the company could go to the directors over their heads. But it was on that principle that Yeats and Lady Gregory had built the Abbey up.

And it would seem that over and above his artistic integrity, and the fact that he was himself a sensitive dramatist, the great merit of Lennox Robinson as producer was that he fitted in so tactfully between company and directors, with his gentle, rather lackadaisical ways. In 1923 he was rewarded with a directorship in his turn. And if he had the defects of his virtues, particularly on the organising side, Lady Gregory was constantly at hand to do the necessary gingering-up. They made a good team, and those who affect to commiserate with him on her interference are, curiously enough, the first to complain that from the time her hand was removed, standards declined.

5

She took her first and only chance of putting her acting theories into practice in March of 1919, when a revival of *Kathleen ni Houlihan* was due, and Maire nic Shiubhlaigh, the Kathleen, suddenly found that she could not appear for the first three nights. Rather than postpone the play, Lady Gregory volunteered to act the part herself; 'after all, what is wanted but a hag and a voice?' As at her first public speaking in America, she felt acutely nervous beforehand, but confident once she was on the stage.

I have talked to two people who remember the performance. To her niece, Ruth Shine, it remains the finest Kathleen she ever saw. She may be considered prejudiced, but Mr Brinsley Macnamara's dispassionate verdict is that it equalled Sara Allgood's interpretation. Lady Gregory seemed, he says, completely to overcome the physical handicap of being small and dumpy; one noticed only the fine carriage of her head and her noble brow.

Maire nic Shiubhlaigh writes of the performance (which of course she did not see) on the slightly sub-acid note she uses to describe all Lady Gregory's doings; but then, she was probably not a little piqued by the amount of publicity her distinguished understudy had received.

6

A biography of Hugh Lane had been early mooted as part of the campaign to get his pictures back for Ireland. It was important to establish in the public mind the contradictory character of a man who could amass a fortune by picture-dealing before he was thirty, yet remain so careless and ignorant of ordinary business procedure as to leave an unwitnessed codicil to his will.

Lady Gregory was asked to undertake the work in 1916, but refused; she felt herself too distracted with anxiety about her son. Another biographer was found, but died before he could do more than amass the relevant papers. It then became evident, she says, that 'the writing of this story of Hugh's life must be done by me or left undone'; also that there were going to be grave delays and difficulties about getting the papers back. Accordingly, she set out to write a book based mainly on her recollections and those of his friends, a 'folk biography' as it might be called — and indeed, she virtually so describes it. She spent a London autumn and an Irish winter interviewing anyone, from 'creators' to gallery caretakers, who could give her an impression, an anecdote, a gesture; 'and when I returned home in the evening I would write down my day's gains, which I had gathered through a memory that had been trained through much gathering of folklore. And this seemed akin to folklore, the tradition coming through many memories, and that come together make a whole.'

Hugh Lane's Life and Achievement: With Some Account of the Dublin Galleries is an intensely personal book, having in it a great deal about herself as well as about Hugh Lane. But this in no way detracts from his portrait, because from the start of his professional career he and she had been allies. He was the member of her family with whom she had most in common;

she found him his first humble job in the art world, she cured him of his social snobbery, she introduced him to the people who were to open his eyes to the French Impressionists, she campaigned fruitlessly to get him a post he coveted (and would have taken for no pay) as curator of the Dublin National Museum; she wore herself out trying to get the gallery built to house his pictures, and trying to keep both him and Dublin in good-humour through the long dispute.

And in the end, as has been seen, she found herself saddled with the legal responsibility of seeing that the fatal codicil was carried out. (He also left her a string of pearls; although so unworldly, she could appreciate fine jewels, and one is happy to think she got something besides frustration from his bequest.)

But even had there been no legal obligation, she could never have rested in the matter of the Lane Pictures, both because she loved her country, and because she loved Hugh Lane. He was bound up with the happiest time of her life, and his gaiety and quickness, his curiosity and sympathy, his lovely London house and generous hospitality, had contributed to that happiness in no small degree. Fragile though he was in build, he had been among her most stalwart supporters at the time of the *Playboy* riots, 'in evening dress and with unruffled shirt-cuffs leading out disturbers of the peace.' 'Of all the ways in which I miss him,' she says, 'perhaps I miss him most as one I laughed with.' And indeed it is always the joke unsharable that hurts most when those we love die young, or young in heart.

Accordingly, her memoir does not read like propaganda, though that it effectively is, but like a deliberate effort of will and memory to recover the bright spirit, and keep it with her still. It is a piece of genuine character-drawing, which suggests that had the Abbey not existed to turn her into a playwright, she might equally have become a novelist.

How dramatic the opening is! — and how brave too, when one remembers that she was writing in 1919, and of people who were her close relations:

'When I sometimes said to Hugh that two lives had been spoiled, been squandered, for his making, I said it half in jest. And yet in pondering as to where he came from, where his roots were, how that daring imagination and amazing fulfilment found its place in the line of a county family of Galway, a professional family of Cork, it sometimes seems to me that I did not exaggerate, that a clash between opposing natures had been needed to create such a fiery current, that the force which enabled him to accomplish in his shortened life so much that will endure, could have come from no other wellhead than that romantic unhappy marriage, that ill-mated parentage.'

His was almost a split personality because he was the child of two people who should never have married; that is her contention, and she presents her evidence with remarkable detachment and fairness to both sides. As usual, it is Mrs Persse who is the villainess of the piece. Her snobbery and prejudice kept apart the high-minded, 'evangelical' Adelaide and the ambitious worldly divinity student during the two years when they ought to have been getting to know each other better, and finding their mutual unsuitability out. They married as strangers, and if Lane senior was something of a social climber, he was also intelligent, with a feeling for literature, whereas Adelaide had her full share of the Persse Philistinism.

'She told me long after that once in that long engagement, she had sent him, in place of the forbidden letter, a copy of some poem, a religious one, she thought might please him, and it was not till a few days after their marriage she discovered he had all the time supposed her to be its author. She said: "It was a great disappointment to him; things never went very well with us after that." '

A pathetically revealing detail that Trollope might not have disdained.

But his aunt has missed one factor in the making of Hugh Lane to which any believer in pre-natal influence — and what woman is not? — must surely attach importance. He was born, as she records, in a small house in the south of Ireland, which had been unexpectedly left to his father. What I learn from his sister is that this house was full of family pictures and furniture, some of it of high quality, and that Adelaide was sorting and re-packing it for sale while she waited for the birth of this child. None of her other children showed the smallest interest in, or aptitude for, the arts.

He grew up sensitive and delicate, his mother's darling and resented by father and brothers, arrogantly intelligent and emotionally insecure. The parents separated, and his father contributed no more to his keep after he was eighteen. He began with Colnaghi as little more than an office-boy, but even in that fairytale world of art-dealing the rapidity of his rise was fantastic. He could 'smell' Old Masters under the dingiest varnish, the thickest over-painting.

Among many dramatic stories, one is illustrated in the book with before-and-after reproductions of the picture in question. It came in to Christie's as 'school of Lawrence', and showed a woman in Regency dress, but Lane looked at it and said, 'I cannot be mistaken in those Romney eyes.' He rubbed the dark paint of hair and dress, and pale colours appeared beneath. The portrait was cleaned, and the sitter revealed in the pale gauzy costume, powdered hair and plumed hat of thirty years earlier. And eventually, Romney's receipt for payment was found among the papers of her descendants.

And we are made to feel the same 'over-painting' in the character of Hugh Lane himself; on the surface the smart, get-rich-quick art dealer, and beneath the fey and dedicated spirit, living only, and unselfishly, for beauty. He has very little sense of personal property; he buys to give away, or if he must sell, would rather sell to a public gallery than to a rich collector, for in a gallery 'it is as much mine as ever, I still possess it, I can see it when I like and everyone else can see it too, so there's no waste in the matter'. Best of all he loves to give to a gallery, and so arises the dream of the perfect gallery, which he will give to his native Ireland, its form and its contents equally moulded by his taste.

He never married, and though he had so many and such gifted friends, remained fundamentally solitary and detached. 'I believe,' Gerald Kelly told her, 'he would have killed his whole family, his grandmother — though perhaps not his aunt, he was very fond of you — but certainly he would have killed me and all his friends for the sake of that Dublin Gallery.'

His entertaining was princely, but left to himself he would exist on buns and cups of tea. He was forever recommending cheap restaurants to his Aunt Augusta, who retorted that there was no economy in paying for food you could not eat. The veneer of elegant insincerity which enabled him to handle millionaire customers was stripped away in a flash when any serious principle of art was involved. To some unfortunates who asked his advice on the best place to hang their daughter's portrait by Lázslò, he answered: 'The best place would be in the dark.'

And with all his cocksureness, he was at bottom humble-minded; perhaps it is this that endears him most of all to his aunt, and through her, to us. Many might consider that an aesthetic appreciation as acute as his was in itself creative, but he did not. The real creators were an aristocracy — I hope and believe he felt her to be among them — and those who merely bought, or sold, or viewed, or interpreted their creations might have their usefulness but were forever left outside. He made a revealing comment when someone

N

deplored Synge's early death: 'How foolish to talk of Synge's small volume of work! Why, generations after I, who have created nothing, am dead and forgotten, Ireland will be watching his plays.'

7

But if Hugh Lane emerges from her book as a character we can recognise and understand — more easily, perhaps, than he was understood in his lifetime — still it is difficult to forgive him the carelessness that laid on an aging and gifted woman the fret and strain and wearisomeness of a lost cause. It is hard always to bear in mind that his carelessness was of a piece with his death on the *Lusitania*; that both were the result of pure bad luck.

If only she could have known that it was a lost cause! If she had listened to Bernard Shaw, and turned her attention to more profitable things, instead of letting the last twelve years of her life be rotted by false promises and the heartsickness of hope deferred! But indeed, it did not look lost in 1920. The Irish were now unanimously determined to have the pictures back — Carson, the Ulster leader, was to prove as staunch a campaigner as any — and even in England there was a widespread feeling that they were 'legally England's but morally Ireland's'. Augustus John, Max Beerbohm, William Rothenstein, William Nicholson and many other distinguished English artists supported the Irish claim. The English press were on the whole sympathetic, and there seemed every chance of appealing through it to the English sense of fair play — an attribute, however, in which the Irish have never greatly believed.

But the dog kept the butter in its mouth. Michael Collins, in the negotiations which led to the Peace Treaty and the formation of the Provisional Government, brought up the matter of the Lane Pictures, but without result. Carson raised

it in the House of Lords; this produced, not legislation, but
the appointment of a Committee, to decide whether Lane
thought his codicil had legal force.

It took the Committee nearly two years to debate the point.
They then produced a farcical and shameful report, answering
the question in the affirmative, but adding that 'had he been
spared to witness the growth of the new gallery at Millbank,
no doubt can be entertained that he would have destroyed the
codicil'. The truth was, as the report itself went on injudici-
ously to admit, that Lord Duveen's gift of money to build
the additions to the Tate Gallery had been secretly conditional
on the Lane Pictures being retained.

Finally, Dublin provided its Gallery of Modern Art, partly
built, and partly converted from a noble eighteenth-century
mansion in what is now Parnell Square. Lady Gregory lived
to see the conversion almost completed — but not the Lane
Pictures brought home.

Through almost every *démarche* in the next ten years, she
must be seen as the leading figure — organising, stirring up,
drafting memoranda, writing letters to the papers, enduring
the 'bland side-tracking' of English officials, trudging round
to the houses of the influential, the important, and the self-
important. That is the picture that many still have of her: a
shabby, importunate old woman, badgering them in a lost
cause. But it was a just cause, it was through no fault of her
own that she had to be importunate, and she will be remembered when most of those she badgered are forgotten.

Page after page of her *Journals* is filled with the unending,
soul-killing round — but fortunately it is not a round on
which the literary biographer has the duty of accompanying
her. All I have to ask is: did the fret over the Lane Pictures
interfere with her creative work? And the question has, for
me, already been answered by my belief that the creative
urge always takes precedence, always makes its own right-of-

way. It is true that only one of the plays she wrote after the burden had been laid on her seems to me to be of the first quality; but that is, surely, because she was growing old and her talent was running out. To write even one short play as good as *Dave* at the age of seventy-four is a remarkable achievement — and a lucky one. If she could have got the Lane Pictures back she would have died a happier woman, but I cannot suppose it would have given any fresh spurt to her creative life.

XII

Religious Plays

It is mercifully no part of my duty to chronicle the violence and horror which filled Ireland, first through the Black and Tan War with England, and then through the Civil War, long after most of Europe had healed its wounds. I have only to record that they caused Lady Gregory great anxiety as an Abbey director, and great suffering in her family life, and inevitably affected the tone of the three plays she had still to write.

A curfew was imposed on bullet-riddled Dublin, and the audience which had come back after the war dwindled again; the theatre lost £800 in a year. The company were 'rebelly' as ever, and told with glee a story of their female director walking into a Black and Tan ambush outside the theatre. Her companions threw themselves flat on the pavement, but instead of following their example, she stood there shouting 'Up the rebels!' at the top of her small voice. Finally the curfew hour got down to eight o'clock, and this did for the Abbey what the world war had never done. It had to close and admit defeat.

But only temporary defeat. She was full of plans and courage. 'Anyhow we have both outlived Miss Horniman,' she reminded Yeats in a letter, and again, 'I hope we won't have to give up the Abbey to a cinema as Miss Horniman has done.* I am glad we have outlasted her, and have faith.' The marks of Miss Horniman's claws had gone very deep.

* At the Gaiety in Manchester.

Once again they issued an appeal. Lectures in London were
organised, and this time she could share in the speaking as
well as doing most of the begging. They raised nearly £500,
and then Lady Ardilaun, the good friend who had tided them
through other crises, sent a cheque for a further £500. The
Abbey was safe for the moment, and the young playwright
who was to bring it a fresh lease of life and prosperity was
just around the corner.

But if things were grim in Dublin, they were certainly no
better at Gort. The prosperous little town had less of a
'rebelly' tradition than most places in Ireland, yet it became
the scene of some of the worst Black and Tan outrages. Her
journals for the autumn and winter of 1920–21 record
horrible things done and a countryside terrorised, and her
own anguish at her inability to protect neighbours and
dependants.

H. J. Massingham, editor of the English weekly *The Nation*,
was one of the first journalists to awaken the British public to
the atrocities being committed in its name. The stately
denunciations of his leading articles were vividly illustrated
by excerpts from Lady Gregory's *Journals*, from which one
could learn what happened to the blacksmith's wife and to
the Loughnane boys, and what living in a state of terror
meant to ordinary decent people. The excerpts appeared as
'from an Irish landlord', in order to protect Coole from
reprisals. Those who knew Lady Gregory's style could have
had no difficulty in identifying the writer, but doubtless this
did not include any officer of the Black and Tans.

Crime bred revenge and the victims, often enough, were
innocent; so it happened twice in her family. Her nephew
Frank Shawe-Taylor, brother of John of the Land Purchase
Act, was murdered in an I.R.A. ambush close to his home at
Athenry. The next year, her daughter-in-law, Mrs Robert
Gregory, was the only one to escape with her life when a

carload of five people were ambushed on the estate of her neighbours, the Bagots of Ballyturin. Lady Gregory was in England at the time; the news when it reached her by telegram filled her with horror and she offered to return by the next train. This did not, however, deter the voices which were whispering that she must have known of the ambush beforehand, and that was why her daughter-in-law's life had been spared.

Such calumnies spread, and added to the bitterness of the time. To some of her family, and to many of her own social class outside it, it seemed as though she had denounced the Black and Tan atrocities and was now condoning those of the I.R.A. 'Your Aunt Augusta is hand in glove with the rebels,' the younger generation was told, and forbidden to hold any communication with Coole.

Ascendancy neighbours closed their houses and removed in disgust to England. Life at Coole became one of increasing loneliness, and though the tradition that 'Coole was on the side of the people' continued to protect it when the war with England changed into an even grimmer war between Irishmen, still there were nerve-racking episodes, thumps on the door and threats in the night. 'I felt it was right, somehow, I should know what others had suffered in like cases,' she wrote in her journal. When she met her English-born neighbour, Mrs Bagot, they compared notes with quiet pride; two solitary, aging women who had not run away.

The Civil War left her, like so many other Irish men and women of good will, deeply bewildered. She admired Michael Collins, who had taken up the cause of the Lane Pictures, and his death was a bad blow. But on the other hand, she had always felt that De Valera was the leader who would ultimately bring stability to Ireland. She seems to have based her belief chiefly on feminine intuition and a fancied resemblance between his face and Abraham Lincoln's, but after all,

the course of history was not to prove her wrong. The
Treaty oath which was the technical cause of the war seemed
to her quite unimportant — 'that wretched oath' she calls it
— and certainly not worth the dreadful loss of young life, the
destruction of so much that was beautiful in the old Ireland,
so much that was of promise in the new. She was a Republican,
certainly, but 'a Republican without malice', and longing
chiefly for peace.

And in the end, Roxborough itself went. The reigning
Persse, her nephew Arthur, was an able farmer and a more
popular landlord than any Persse had been for generations,
but that did not save his house from being commandeered by
the I.R.A. in 1922, doubtless because of its strategic position
in the valley. They treated it well, but left it without warning
and without putting in any guard. It is thought that it was
then looted by a gang of marauders, and set on fire to cover
the traces of their thefts.

Only the loss of Coole could have hit her more cruelly.
With her great-niece Kathleen she visited the blackened
roofless house, the garden turning over to grass and weeds,
and rescued some phloxes to enrich her own borders, as in
later years her great-niece would rescue plants from Coole to
be a tiny scrap of Persse gardening surviving in Kent.

And to the end of her life, Roxborough would be a place
of occasional melancholy pilgrimage, and she would think of
Oisin's return to Almhuin: 'for as he was the last of the
Fianna, so am I of my generation, the brothers, the sisters;
and now the homestead that had sheltered us all a deserted
disconsolate ruin.'

2

With so much violence and suffering around her, it is not
surprising that her thoughts should turn to the supreme
suffering, the betrayal and death of Christ. Her first play had

been a religious one, and even in those pre-Abbey days, Father Hegarty, a friend of Yeats and AE, had suggested the writing of an Irish Passion Play as a worthy objective for the new dramatic movement. Yeats urged her, as the orthodox believer of the group, to attempt it, but as she says in her note to the play, 'It was only last summer (1923), when my life seemed to have drifted into a quiet backwater, and I was much alone, that the great subject took hold of me, and so filled my mind that I was forced to get it into words, and into the form I am most used to, of a play.'

But if the idea came from a Catholic source, and the result proved most happily acceptable to Catholic opinion, it must not on that account be imagined that Lady Gregory was ever anything but the staunchest of Protestants. There is, her family assure me, no truth at all in Yeats's insinuation that she flirted with the notion of turning Catholic in order to get closer to the people; and indeed it would be quite out of character. She was, one may say, Protestant by temperament, and would surely have gravitated towards the mild and tolerant independence of thought represented by the best elements in the Church of Ireland, even if she had not been born and brought up in it — quite as inevitably as the doctrinaire temperament of a Maud Gonne led her to the Church of Rome. The Bible-readings and learnings by heart of Roxborough had left her mind impregnated with biblical thought. It was one of the first things that she and Sean O'Casey, apparently from so different a world, found they had in common.

The losing religion, for such it already was in her day, further made a strong emotional appeal to her sense of loyalty. She had an almost maternal tenderness for the forlorn churches, the tiny congregations, the clergy islanded in a sea of Catholicism. If she could return to Galway today, her heart would bleed at the last stages in the Protestant defeat:

churches locked or derelict, or so completely gone that there is not even a stone to mark where they stood.

Her religious sense was deep, and she had great faith in the power of prayer, but it was feeling, not doctrine, that mattered to her. The last nine years had tragically emphasised the futility of hatred as a motive force in human affairs, the absolute necessity of replacing it by love. And this is the message which, in *The Story Brought by Brigit*, she is trying to communicate.

But there are formidable difficulties in the writing of a play based on the New Testament. There would seem to be three methods: to transcribe literally, as is done at Oberammergau; to transcribe into contemporary terms, as Miss Dorothy Sayers did in her radio plays; or to present a reflection of the biblical story on the minds and experiences of imaginary characters. This last is, I suspect, the only means whereby the artist can really add anything of aesthetic value. Lady Gregory's play combines the first and last methods, and inevitably the two do not quite coalesce.

Those parts of it which are 'reflection' are remarkably successful. Language presents no problem. 'Kiltartan', at once homely and poetic, seems completely appropriate for the sorrowing women of Jerusalem, for the fickle rabble and for the patriotic mountainy boy. The parallel between Roman-occupied Palestine and English-occupied Ireland emerges naturally and impressively. To Joel, the boy, Jesus is a political liberator, and he loses heart when it seems that after all the Leader's triumph is not to be of this world.

All the 'political' characters are good. Marcus, Pilate's right-hand man, is the decent Ascendancy official, by no means dead to justice or unable to recognise courage, but grown cynical through years of handling the bigot and the hypocrite. 'To tell the clean truth, a little Rising now and then is no harm at all. It gives us an excuse to get rid of disturbers and to bring more of our armies in. A Rising too is very apt to lead to splits, and splits are a great help when you want to keep a country down.'

Silas, a scribe in the pay of Caiaphas, is the typical self-righteous traditionalist, with a cunning that defeats its own ends. Daniel, the tinker, is taken from the folk-tradition that makes tinkers outcasts because one of them drove the nails through Our Lord's hands and feet, when a Roman soldier flinched from the task. He is the genial drunken ruffian who makes up part of every Irish mob, and appears harmless and even rather engaging till one looks more closely, and sees something horrible beneath.

Against the four men, doomed to be vessels of violence and error, are set the gracious sorrowing figures of St Brigit and the three Women of Jerusalem, with their exquisite keen, taken (with some little alteration) from one in Douglas Hyde's *Religious Songs of Connacht*. Had she been able to diversify and strengthen the women to the point where they could stand against the male characters, and derive the whole of her action from the conflict so personified between political violence and human pity, she could, I think, have produced a dramatic commentary on the Crucifixion which would have been in itself completely satisfying.

She has not quite done this; nor, in bringing on the actual figures of Our Lord, the Virgin and St John, has she brought herself to paraphrase the Gospel words they speak. Admittedly their appearances are brief, but the dramatic illusion of an Irish Passion Play is broken.

The Story Brought by Brigit must accordingly be adjudged a work of piety rather than a work of art. The Abbey put it on in Holy Week of 1924 (the next new production after *Juno and the Paycock*), and the restless cynical Dublin audience seems to have been deeply impressed by it, but its proper home is no doubt the specifically religious stage. Nevertheless it contains far more imaginative life than most works of dramatic piety, and its tenderness, its anguished sense of physical and mental suffering, are the answer to those who still maintain that Lady Gregory was the sort of rebel for whom the means justify the end.*

3

The wish to write a Don Quixote play had likewise been long in her mind. She had her own quixotic streak, which responded to forlorn hopes and lost causes and the sort of heroism that does not count the cost, and at this juncture Quixote's selfless idealism seemed more than ever lovely in her eyes. But precisely for this reason, the theme was not really one that fitted her. She could not bring to it the requisite streak of Spanish cruelty. The Irish dramatist who could have re-created Cervantes' great figure was not Lady Gregory, but Synge.

Sancho's Master has nobility and tenderness, but it is not funny, and in consequences long portions of it fall flat. Even Sancho is unamusing compared with the preliminary sketch of him she had made in *The Golden Apple*. She has tried, moreover, to work in too many incidents. The problem of construction was becoming increasingly difficult in these last years.

In the much simpler, one-act *Dave*, however, she has at last, or so it seems to me, got her religious message into a genuine dramatic form, and achieved a modern miracle play. There is nothing clever or metaphysical about it, but the characters have life, and so the message has validity.

* On my last visit to Ireland, I found a renewal of interest in the religious writings of Lady Gregory, and particularly in this play. It was pointed out that a country so preoccupied with religion ought not to be so poor in religious drama, and there were suggestions for either reviving *Brigit* or adapting it. My own feeling is that if performed as part of a religious festival, it would be effective as it stands.

Once again it cost her great pains. She struggled with it over a long period, hampered by increasing ill-health. At first she entangled herself with her old enemy, the supernatural: the message was to be brought by a Ragged Woman, an angel unawares. She read the draft to Yeats, who rightly objected to this figure, but as usual could make no constructive suggestion. The clue came from Lennox Robinson, the practising playwright. Why not, he said, give the message to Kate, the farmer's wife, who was already shown in a sympathetic relationship to Dave? And she at once perceived that this, and not the message itself, was the miracle — this capacity of weak and stupid people suddenly to rise to a crisis where the knowing and the efficient have failed.

Much study has been given by social workers in recent years to the problem of the 'deprived child'. But this pathetic figure had not been isolated under the sociological microscope in 1926, and what Lady Gregory knew about Dave, she knew from her observation of the orphans in the Gort Workhouse, and by her natural lights. Dave is an adolescent foundling, used as slave-labour in the household of the rich farmer Nicholas, not actively ill-treated, but robbed of individual dignity and blamed for everything that goes wrong. He does not even own a surname; he is 'Dave, short and sharp like you would shout for a dog'. The contempt of those around him has made him surly and brutal, and no one takes his part but Kate, Nicholas's wife, who is too much in awe of her socially superior husband to be effective.

The resentments smouldering in Dave keep him close to hysteria, and on very small provocation it breaks out into violence. Nicholas and the steward overpower and bind him, and rush out to find the Sheriff, leaving him in Kate's charge. At first she too is frightened; then, as she watches the half-unconscious boy, pity and a sense of shame for what has been done to him flood her. She washes the blood from his head and cuts his cords, and begs Heaven's blessing upon him. And the sense of being loved and valued at last penetrates the boy's misery and heals him. He sees in a vision the life he might have, as giver and succourer, no longer as the object of others' charity. 'A very laughable thing,' he tells Kate as he comes out of his dream. 'It was nearly like as if I was a king's son or a great gentleman. I could not but laugh thinking that.'

When Nicholas and the steward return, they find him free and sane, no longer concerned with them or his grievances, but seeking a direction for his life. A chance word gives it to him — people are dying of famine-fever in Connemara. 'Those are the ones I will go to!' he cries, and takes up his spade. 'If it should fail me to earn a handful of meal to keep the life in them, I can show service to the dead. Those that die on the roadside I will not leave to be dragged by a dog, or swallowed down a boghole.' And when Kate protests that he is not yet well enough, he tells her: 'I give you my word I never felt so merry or so strong. I am like one that has found his treasure and must go share it with his kin. Why wouldn't I be airy, doing that?'

After he has gone, Kate understands that love has gone out out of her house and her life, and even Nicholas is shaken out of his self-satisfaction. He offers to call the boy back and make him rich, but Kate replies: 'I wouldn't ask it. God has surely some great hand in him. He had the look of being very glad in the mind. His head held high, and a light on his brow as bright as the bow of heaven. May friends and angels be around him and steer him to a good harbour in the Paradise of the King!'

Those last words of blessing were the last words of a Gregory character on the stage. She was pleased with the play's reception at the Abbey, the dead silence all through the mystic part, the applause at the end, the appreciation of AE to whom it was dedicated (the idea of the peasant-saint being taken from one of his poems), and a word of praise from Yeats himself. But she made a sensible resolve 'not to tempt my luck again'.

She translated one more Molière play, as *The Would-Be Gentleman*, but it is a literal translation, with nothing of her own beyond a slight pruning of the French text. It, *Dave* and *Sancho's Master* were published together in 1928 as *Three Last Plays*, and she says of the title: 'My decision that these three plays — or two, with one translation — must be my last has been made without advice save from the almanac, and rather from pride than modesty.' It was a good idea to end on a success; not, to be sure, the surging thunderous success of an O'Casey, but the gentle satisfaction of one who had listened to the voice of her own suffering, and at last found words to express what it had taught her.

XIII

Sean O'Casey

━━━━━━◦◦◦◦✦◦◦◦◦━━━━━━

I

As an organiser, Lady Gregory earned her richest reward
from the discovery of Sean O'Casey. This is not, of
course, to say that without her he would have remained
unknown. Gifts as striking as his could never have been
passed over, and in fact Yeats and Lennox Robinson were
equally alive to them. But she was the first to discern them
through the fumbling of his early efforts, and she was the only
one of the Abbey group to secure his friendship, and to give
him the sympathy which was far more important to his
development than any amount of criticism or technical hints.

He came at the right moment, just after the Abbey had
been saved by the curfew appeal of 1921, and was looking
anxiously for new talent. In November of that year, she
puzzled out the manuscript of a play called *The Crimson in
the Tricolour*, written on poor paper and in worse ink, and
was so struck by it that she sent a long critical note to the
author. Later, after Yeats had decided against producing it,
she summoned him for a personal interview. 'Your strong
point is characterisation,' she told him. Not, one would
think, a startlingly original observation, but apparently it was
just what he needed to deflect him from the axe-grinding and
grievance-airing that have been the ruin of so much Irish
creative talent.

He took it to heart, went back to his bed-sittingroom, and
wrote a play in which the revolutionary background is used

merely to reveal the weak spots in character; and with *The Shadow of a Gunman* (1923) he and the Abbey romped home to the biggest success since the first night of *Blanco Posnet*. And it was the very success that Yeats and Lady Gregory had dreamed of and planned for — the young proletarian genius, untouched by outside influences, who should put the speech and the soul of working-class Dublin on to the stage.

O'Casey saved the Abbey more permanently and effectively than Lady Ardilaun had done, but he was not on that account personally its whiteheaded boy. On his own admission he was touchy and difficult, at once arrogantly sure of his gifts and bristling with social inferiority-complex, stiffnecked and bitterly poor. He disliked Lennox Robinson, and felt himself patronised by Yeats. He had his own views on acting and production — which after all were his prerogative, for had it not always been a dramatist's theatre? But the company which had accepted, if not always with meekness, the dictatorship of Yeats, Synge and Lady Gregory was not prepared to be taught its business by Sean O'Casey with the cement still on his hands. His initial bewilderment with the new feuds and faces surrounding him turned all too rapidly to antagonism. Only with 'the Old Lady' did he feel himself at home.

From the first they were friends, and it is easy to see that on each side there was an emotional bias over and above their common interest in the theatre. He was still grieving for his mother, and she for her son. Each found in the other a substitute for the lost outlet, and their idyllic relationship inspires the happiest pages in her *Journals*, and in the fourth volume of his autobiography, *Inishfallen, Fare Thee Well*.

His physical description of her is a Rembrandt portrait in words:

'A sturdy, stout little figure soberly clad in solemn black, made gay with a touch of something white under a long, soft, black

o

silk veil that covered her grey hair and flowed gracefully behind half-way down her back. A simple brooch shyly glistened under her throat, like a bejewelled lady making her first retreat, feeling a little ashamed of it. Her face was a rugged one, hardy as that of a peasant, curiously lit with an odd dignity, and softened with a careless touch of humour in the bright eyes and the curving wrinkles crowding around the corners of the firm little mouth. She looked like an old, elegant nun of a new order, a blend of the Lord Jesus Christ and of Puck, an order that Ireland had never known before, and wasn't likely to know again for a long time to come.'

Her Dublin headquarters at this time was the Russell Hotel, and here, or in the Abbey green-room, she drew out of him the story of his aspirations and heartbreaks, as she had done with so many young writers. But this time it was not a one-sided process, for she had at last found the friend sensitive enough to appreciate her qualities in his turn.

'They got on grand together. They had many things in common besides the theatre. He loved pictures, and she was brimful of what her nephew, Hugh Lane, had done to diamond-clothe the walls of precious buildings. . . . She loved good books, and Sean felt he was a little ahead of her there. She saw humour sparkle from things thought to be dead, or dull, and so did he; and they often talked and laughed together over tea in a hotel that overlooked the fair form of Stephen's Green, Sean trying to look at home in the posh place, and succeeding in a way; she eating bun after bun, murmuring that she was very, very hungry; and saying that their talk was lovely; though best of all, she rejoiced that his plays were forcing queues to stand outside her little theatre; ringing a chime of cheeriness into all their chat.'

Juno and the Paycock (1924) fulfilled all she had predicted for him. No reservations here, no half-praise, as with Synge; she wrote in her *Journal*: 'A wonderful and terrible play of futility, of irony, humour, tragedy,' and after the performance she told Yeats: 'This is one of the evenings at the Abbey which make me glad to have been born.'

2

In June he received the accolade of an invitation to Coole. He was nervous and apprehensive as he travelled down to the junction at Athenry, but she was waiting for him there, and they proceeded to Gort in a crowded third-class carriage:

'Look at her there, with all her elegance, well at ease among the chattering crowd of common people; so why shouldn't I be steady in my mind coming to a Big House, among rare silver and the best of china, sleeping in a bounteous bed, and handling divers tools at food never seen before? And he took heart, and felt strong, looking at the calm handsome old face, smiling at the chatter of the people and the frightened cackling of the fowl.'

The Coole side-car met them, and when they reached the house:

'she showed her Connacht rearing by compelling her seventy-odd years to climb down, like a stiff gazelle, from the high seat of the side-car, running to the threshold of the house, turning, and stretching out her two hands to say, with a beaming smile, One and twenty welcomes, Sean, to the House of Coole!'

Unsophisticated as he was, even he could see that by this time there was nothing very grand about Coole. It was comfortably shabby without and within; a Big House, but 'dying reluctantly, filled a little too full with things brought from all quarters of the known world'. Best of all he relished 'the really glorious library, walled with precious books in calf and vellum, forgotten, the most of them'. Here by candlelight she improved his mind by reading aloud from Hardy's *Dynasts* (which sent him to sleep), and they experimented with a wonderful new petrol lamp, which was to make all bright as day. But it blew up, and they returned gratefully to the peace and security of the candles.

Nor did the 'divers tools at food' prove much of a hurdle:

'He hadn't been ten minutes at the table before he felt that he had often been there, to eat soberly, and talk merrily of books and the theatre, and of the being of Ireland; she in simple and most gracious ways showing how things were handled; pointing out that these things were done, not because of any desire for ceremony, but because they made one more comfortable, and made things easier to eat.'

They walked in the Seven Woods, she with gauntleted hands and a chisel-edged stick, stabbing out thistles and uprooting ivy with cries of *So perish all the king's enemies!* She taught him to distinguish between the trees, for he hardly knew oak from elm, beech, hazel or pine. It was the first time he had ever stayed in a place where he was allowed to pick the flowers.

He watched her handling tenants and dependants, signing pension papers for an old man on a wet day, and sending him away with a gift of the brandy that was supposed to go into the current barmbrack. 'With all her bowing-down before the mystery of poetry and painting, she never left the sober paths trod into roughness by the feet of the common people.'

'He is very happy walking in the woods,' she noted in her diary, but he confesses that he found too much of them oppressive. He was happier on the open hillside, alive with blue butterflies, or in the garden at evening, where as the sun went down he pondered on her part in the Irish Renascence:

'... crying out in her quiet, determined way through all the mumbo-jamboree of twilight thought, that there were things to cook, sheets to sew, pans and kettles to mend ... this woman who, in the midst of venomous opposition, served as a general runabout in sensible pride and lofty humility, crushing time out of odd moments to write play after play that kept life passing to and fro on the Abbey stage.... In the theatre, among the poets and playwrights, herself a better playwright than most of them, she acted the part of a charwoman, but one with a star on her breast.'

And then follows the outburst against Yeats, for his persistent destroying of her creative confidence, which I have already quoted.

At the end of this most happy visit, they travelled back to Dublin together. There was the inevitable wait at Athenry, and he wandered off to look at the town and the Abbey ruins (and a bit of skirt). Returning, he caught her unawares, nodding her head over *Peg O' My Heart* in the station waiting-room. One who admires her nearly as much as I do, but him rather less, considers it a disloyalty on his part to have betrayed his friend's weakness for the lighter literature, but I do not think he intended it so. He is presentingly her lovingly, in the round. Nor do I find anything strange in her wish to examine the text of a work in which her beloved Sara Allgood had scored a personal success far greater than any achieved, alas, in the masterpieces of herself or Synge. And while there might have been something a shade unsuitable about reading *Peg O' My Heart* in Coole library, I can testify that no such objection applies to that intrinsically dreary spot, the station waiting-room at Athenry.

3

Before the next O'Casey play, *The Plough and the Stars*, was produced, the Abbey had become the first state-subsidised theatre in the English-speaking world. It is a development for which Yeats and Lady Gregory have been blamed — or rather, for which she has been blamed, since it is usual, as I have already noted, to minimize Yeats's part when criticisms are flung around. And she may well have been more whole-hearted in the matter than he was, since she was the director who did the worrying, who was continually aware, in the words of the representation she made to the Minister of Finance, of 'our actors underpaid, our actor-manager getting only £6–7 a week, our building so shabby and wanting repair'.

But Yeats, when it came to practical matters of hard cash, was quite as level-headed as herself, and none of the critics seem able to suggest what alternative they had. The theatre knew brief periods of affluence, as in America, and now in the O'Casey boom, but experience had proved that with its small seating capacity and boldly experimental policies it could not, over the years, really pay its way. The directors had pulled it through recurrent financial crises, the one by his prestige and his drawing-power as a lecturer, the other by her gift for cajoling money out of the well-to-do; but what was to happen when they were gone? They could not legislate to replace themselves, or manufacture other personalities as strong and devoted as they had been, and they could not control the policies of the Abbey from the grave. State money at least ensured that the theatre would physically continue. The modest subsidy (it began at only £850 a year) was given without conditions and strings, and as long as they were at the helm they could resist all oblique pressure. After that the Abbey must take its chance.

But of course, when money is paid over, there are always unspoken conditions and invisible strings, no matter how disinterested the original intention. A significant day in February of 1925 was spent by Lady Gregory, first joyously increasing the actors' and charwomen's pay from the Government grant, and then calling on Ernest Blythe, the Minister of Finance, to thank him for it. Mr Blythe recommended that the Abbey should take on another director, a Catholic, and suggested Dr George O'Brien. He accordingly joined the board, and was in effect, even if not officially, the Government's nominee.

Trouble was not long in coming. The manuscript of *The Plough and the Stars* was received, and Dr O'Brien at once took exception to a great deal in it — the love-scene in the first act, the introduction of a prostitute, the song she was to sing, and violence of language throughout. His tactfully-worded letter to Yeats had its sting in the tail: 'Not being a dramatic author or critic, I feel that the only assistance of value I can render is by attempting to prevent the outbreak of a movement or hostility that would make it difficult or impossible for the Government to continue or to increase its subsidy.'

Lady Gregory comments in her Journal: 'It was after I had read this I said, If we have to choose between the subsidy and our freedom, it is our freedom we choose. "Not an author or a dramatic critic" — we are asked to submit, rather than to the hands of the fruitful, to the mercies of the barren.' It is a revealing admission. The theatre had always been in the hands of the 'fruitful', the creators. By permitting the inclusion of O'Brien on the board, the directors had allowed the rot to set in.

However, their combined strength of personality won the immediate tussle. After two directors' meetings, and the making of sundry minor concessions such as the omission of the streetwalker's song, *The Plough and the Stars* went through, and was presented for the first time on February 8th, 1926. There was some rioting, with which Yeats dealt efficiently and which she was spared, since she was at Coole and did not see the play till the following week, when the worst of the trouble had died down.

In view of the accusations of prudery that have sometimes been levelled at her, it is well to record her profound appreciation of what is in many people's view (and certainly in mine) O'Casey's greatest play. For it is a good deal easier to sympathise with Dr O'Brien and his fellow objectors than with the *Playboy* rioters. *The Plough and the Stars* was tough going for 1926, and it is not a play for the squeamish, even today.

But she took it in her stride. 'A very wonderful play,' she wrote after she had seen it for the second time, 'the forgiveness of sins, as real literature is supposed to be. These quarrelling, drinking women have tenderness and courage, showing all through, as have the men. . . . And then comes what all nations have seen, the suffering that falls through war, and especially civil war, on the women, the poor, the wretched homes and families of the slums. An overpowering play. I felt at the end of it as if I should never care to look at another; all others would seem so shadowy to the mind after this.'

4

And in a sense, she never did 'look at another'. The fulfilment that came to her from *The Plough and the Stars* was the last great experience of her Abbey director's career.

O'Casey, by now hopelessly at odds with literary Dublin, shook the dust of his native land from his feet and emigrated to London; on her next Dublin visit she missed him sadly, but the friendship remained staunch. For a time his genius lay fallow. Then in March of 1928 the Abbey received the manuscript of *The Silver Tassie*, and she a private letter telling her that he thought it the best work he had yet done.

In due course the text reached her with Lennox Robinson's doubts and criticisms, and in the main she agreed with them. Yeats in his turn concurred, in a letter which seemed to her so full of force and integrity that she copied it out and sent it straight to O'Casey. It would give him, she thought, the chance to emend the play before he sent it to the printers. But as she was soon to acknowledge, it was a fatally tactless move.

O'Casey was furious. His astonishment and chagrin were aggravated by what was in his eyes 'a letter of condemnation peppered with pompous advice' from a man whose dramatic abilities, and certainly success, were nothing beside his own. He broke with the Abbey, which then formally rejected the play, and it had its first production in London. And he broke with Lady Gregory, a loss which was very grievous to her, and which, unlike the others she suffered in these last years of her life, was largely her own fault.

For there was an undeniable failure of aesthetic sympathy in her first estimate of *The Silver Tassie*, and she was not long in admitting it. A letter from Bernard Shaw, telling her roundly that she and Yeats had been extremely foolish, and should have accepted the play 'as a calamity imposed by the Act of God', gave her her first jolt; and when she saw it in London, despite the inadequacies of English acting, she repented altogether. 'I am convinced we ought to have taken it and done our best to put it on, and made such cuts of the bad language as he would allow.'

One is still puzzled to explain this myopia that simultaneously afflicted herself, Yeats and Lennox Robinson, who between them had championed so much that was new, difficult or disquieting. There are faults in *The Silver Tassie*; I think it will be generally conceded that the poetic 'chanting' scene in the trenches neither advances the acting nor tones with the realism of the rest. But this was not what they objected to — on the contrary, their continual hankering after poetic drama biassed them in the scene's favour.

Their disapproval was concentrated on the last two acts, in which, she complained, 'the persons are lost in rowdiness.' But it is not so at all. The hospital with its callous flirting nurses, and then the cheap little suburban orgy, throw into livid relief the once-splendid young human animal reduced by his war wounds to crippled impotence, crashing in his wheel-chair on to the ballroom floor, and clawing at the woman he can no longer use. It is appalling, certainly; 'literally a hell of a play', as Shaw said; but if it were less than appalling, it would fail of its purpose, which is to be among the most powerful indictments of war ever set on the stage.

It was not in Lady Gregory to repent without making apology and amends. She wrote again to Sean O'Casey, begging to be allowed to visit him in London, and meet his wife and his baby son. He would not receive her, and they never met again. In his turn he has repented generously of his rejection, but still advances the reason he then gave her, that he would have distressed her by saying hard things about the other two.

Can it be, perhaps, that in this Mr O'Casey deceives himself? One can hardly believe that once his professional indignation had died down he cared a fig for the opinions of Yeats and Lennox Robinson, because he had never liked them, nor they him. But he carried as a lasting scar his sense of injury against Lady Gregory, because he had been fond of her, and she had failed him.

XIV

'The Evening of my Days'

———————◦◦◦◦✦◦◦◦◦◦———————

I

One of the sad things about living to venerable age is that one lives on as old in the public memory. And if a Wordsworth, who did his best work before he was forty, is pictured by us now as permanently elderly, how much more must this be true of a late developer like Lady Gregory. To those who were young when she was old, she tended to appear formidable, unless, like her grandson Richard, her nephew Desmond Shawe-Taylor or Sean O'Casey, they were close to her by blood or sympathy.

'I met her twice only,' says Gerard Fay, 'both times at the theatre when I was playing a small part in *The Hour-Glass*. She was so like Queen Victoria (to my eyes) that I almost called her Your Majesty. And the fantasy was not too far-fetched, for she had a queenly way with her and she ruled the Abbey for years.' The same regal impression was received by Micheal MacLiammoir, who says in his autobiography *All for Hecuba*: 'Although the gentle frosty dignity, as of some royal personage, never left her manner, she was always kind, always courteous, always encouraging.'

To one who knows her only through her *Journals*, it is difficult to fit this stately exterior to the so human, and often in her last years so lonely, woman beneath; still very ready to make friends where she could find them, and wistfully missing the great days of her companionship with Yeats. There is a revealing entry in 1926: 'When I am too long without a friend at hand to talk with I feel, not lonely, but insincere — never speaking my whole mind. In London one touches now and again some part of a mind that is akin. Perhaps some day suddenly again a barrier will go down and I will have made a friend.' Not that she had ever lost Yeats; his marriage had made no difference to the quality of their comradeship; but inevitably it meant that he had less time to give her, though he continued to spend some part of each summer at Coole.

If the barriers went down less and less easily, it was partly because her natural shyness was reinforced by the diffidence of old age, and partly because she was being gradually imprisoned in an ailing body. Arthritis had fastened on her in her sixties, and now in her seventies increasing deafness cut her off from general conversation, and a grimmer enemy declared itself. In September of 1926 she underwent a cancer operation. The enemy was routed, and she had six more years to live, but she was never really robust again.

In mind and awareness, she remained young. There is none of that harking back to good old days, that unfavourable comparing of present with past, that one takes almost for granted in the candid reminiscences of septuagenarians. There is none of old age's self-absorption. If she is nervous about her health, it is only from dread of being a burden to others. Those who met her agree that she always wished to draw them out, to listen to them, not to talk herself. Sean O'Casey did not draw her into reminiscence till he had come to know her well.

In the theatre, she was always on the side of novelty and experiment. The legend has grown up that the title of Denis Johnston's play *The Old Lady Says No* referred to its rejection by Lady Gregory at the Abbey. But the author states (and the text of the play makes clear) that the Old Lady is Ireland, and Lennox Robinson confirms that the play's rejection was due not to Lady Gregory, who admired it, but to Yeats and himself. Dr Robinson further says that he never used the ugly appellation of 'the Old Lady', or thought of her as old. But there is no doubt that it was current among the younger people at the Abbey, though never used, of course, to her face.

This inward youthfulness may, indeed, be in some measure responsible for the feeling of slight alarm she created. It startled people; it was not what they expected from a revered relic of the immediate literary past. They were made uncomfortable by her bright penetrating gaze.

A friend of long standing wrote to J. M. Hone: 'My impression of her eyes, which were most remarkable, was that of intense enquiry behind her glasses, for she was exceedingly short-sighted. Her eyes were enquiring, sarcastic, penetrating, appraising, observant. . . .' Micheal MacLiammoir confirms this picture. Her fine rosy skin, coiled white hair and benevolent pouter-pigeon features were, he says, so much what one is used to in elderly women of good family that automatically one fitted to them vague and gentle blue or grey eyes. Instead one met, and never forgot, those fiercely observant eyes of a curious bright brown.

Her creative time was past and she could make no more use of what she learned, but she did not on that account shut up shop, as most of us do. She went on learning to the end.

2

When he reached undergraduate independence, Desmond Shawe-Taylor, son of the murdered Frank, broke through the family embargo on Coole and made friends with his great-aunt. He had seen the Abbey players in London, and wrote to her enthusiastically. She replied, delighted to find a kindred spirit among the youngest generation of Persses, and invited him to Coole in July of 1927, when the company consisted of herself, her younger granddaughter and Yeats.

Like Sean O'Casey before him, he was enchanted to find himself in a house of books and treasures and deep-rooted culture. It seemed to him almost the setting of a Tchekov play, with Yeats as the typical Tchekovian *ami de la maison*. To him there was nothing in the least formidable about his great-aunt, but her hands were crippled with rheumatism, and Yeats acted as her secretary, writing many letters to her dictation. (It is good to know that the service she had so often rendered him was thus graciously returned.) In the evenings there were the readings-aloud which had always been a feature of life at Coole. The reading this time was done by Yeats, and Trollope's *The American Senator* was his rather unexpected choice.

Desmond Shawe-Taylor continued to correspond with his great-aunt, and deeply regrets that he did not repeat his visit, but an increasing interest in music drew him to the Continent for his long vacations. At least he saw Coole still in Gregory possession. By October of that year it had passed away from the family for ever.

A word should in fairness be said about the ownership of Coole. The country-house which Lady Gregory had made the most famous in Ireland was never legally hers. From Sir William Gregory it passed to his son Robert, and from Robert to his widow Margaret. The Robert Gregorys, whose artistic interests and friends lay chiefly in London and Paris, preferred to spend most of their time there, as Sir William had done before them, treating Coole merely as a holiday home. For this reason, and also because they knew how much it meant to her, they refused Lady Gregory's offer to leave it on their marriage, and she continued to be mistress there, as before.

It was not a self-supporting farming estate, and even in Robert Gregory's lifetime outlying portions of the woods had had to be sold to meet taxation, which became much heavier under the Free State Government. To the grand-children it was a place of dearly loved holidays, but they too had no wish to settle there permanently, and Richard Gregory had decided on a career in the British Army, which would take him far from Ireland. Parting with Coole was a grief to them all, but the final step was planned to be as little painful to Lady Gregory as possible. It was sold to the Forestry Department of the Irish Land Commission, with the proviso that she should continue to occupy house and gardens at a low rent.

But, perhaps inevitably, the situation presented itself rather differently to Lady Gregory. To her it seemed that she was making a long fight, on very little money, to keep Coole going for her grandchildren's sake, and that her efforts were being frustrated. Clear-sighted and ruthless with herself over everything else, she does in this one matter of Coole seem to have given way to some self-deception and wishful-thinking. And when after her death her *Journals*, with their frank revelation of her day-to-day hopes and struggles, came into the possession of her family, they were the cause of some understandable posthumous bitterness.

3

She had renounced playwriting, and she stuck sensibly to her decision, but it was none the less bitter to her. Far worse than any physical loneliness in these last years was the loneli-ness of no longer having living characters jostle each other inside her imagination. She had enjoyed doing the occasional non-fiction book as a change from writing plays, but now that it was the only literary work on hand, she tended to lose heart. 'As I've just written to Huntington,* I feel it rather a come-down writing articles instead of plays, creation in an inverse method to Genesis. But I can't take to idleness of mind,

---

* John Huntington, a director of Messrs. Putnam & Co., Ltd., her publishers.

one wants some creation going on in the background to keep it sweet and sane.'

The 'articles' were a series of essays on Coole, inside and out, which she had written some years before and which she now forced herself to revise, in order to preserve something of a house which had left its mark on literary history — a house which, as she pretty well knew, would be dismantled after her death. In the end only two chapters were completed, on the library and on the garden. Miss Yeats brought them out as *Coole*, a Cuala Press booklet, in 1931, and they constituted the last work published in Lady Gregory's lifetime.

Brief though the book is, it contains some of her most evocative descriptions, and it is a great pity she had not energy to do more. The atmosphere and strangeness of the house in the forest emerge more clearly than in Yeats's poems, (which is not, of course, to criticise them, since she is aiming at the particular and he at the universal). There are attractive vignettes of him, putting his hand on a badger in the remoteness of the woods, planning his plays, wrestling with his poems, as he paced the gravelled walk by the long flower-border, 'I stealing a pleasant half-hour with him between the ordering of the day's meals and the needless answering of letters that falls to a woman's share.' She always writes of him on exactly the right note, warm and admiring yet comradely and brisk. Fellow-visitors to Coole may sometimes have felt he was a little tin god there, but there is no sign of this adulation in any of her autobiographical writings.

There is further news of the Autograph Tree, to which the initials of Sean O'Casey had been added since she introduced it in *Our Irish Theatre*. Unfortunately there were unsolicited contributions too. Several country lads working in the orchard had added theirs, and she had only just been in time to restrain the penknives of some American boy guests. 'It may

Under the catalpa tree. A photograph taken by a Bord Failte photographer in August 1927.

be that I was too rash, that some day in that wonder-country there may be signed by a President in the White House the letters of a name that I had disallowed.' One is tempted to remind her that if that ill-advised tree stood for anything, it stood for literary, not for political or historical, immortality.

Somewhere in her *Journals* she speaks of Coole's 'heartache and loneliness', but in this exquisite little epilogue, only love for it remains, and gratitude to the husband who had brought her there forty-eight years before. 'I have gone far out into the world,' she concludes, 'east and west in my time, and so the peace within these enclosing walls is fitting for the evening of my days.'

4

Up to 1930 she continued to come regularly to Dublin and keep an eye on the Abbey; then her strength began to fail. Her grandson's coming-of-age found her resigned: '. . . it is a contrast to Robert's coming-of-age, with the gathering of cousins and the big feast and dance for the tenants — Coole no longer ours. But the days of landed property have passed. It is better so.' She thought calmly and cheerfully of death, 'so much easier to face than another operation'. When she knew that Coole was to go out of the family, she had had the family vault bricked up. By her own wish she would lie, not beside Sir William, but beside her favourite sister Arabella in the Protestant plot of the new cemetery in Galway, an unromantic spot, sensible and municipal. The great aim was to be no more trouble to anybody than one could help.

The last visit to make literary history was of Yeats and George Russell, 'AE', in the summer of 1931, to discuss the formation of an Irish Academy of Letters.

For a long time she resisted fiercely all attempts to help out her strength. She got herself about the house and garden with a stick. John Diviney, her gardener, recalls her falling and

P

being unable to get to her feet without his aid, and beseeching him to say nothing about it. But in the autumn she was persuaded to have a resident nurse, who shared the task of caring for her with her devoted housekeeper. Her family, then living near Dublin, gave her as much time as they could, and so did Yeats.

She was failing gently all through the winter and spring, with little pain — a merciful dispensation, since she never would consent to take any pain-killing drugs that might deaden the mind. One day in March she had herself helped for the last time all round the house, saying goodbye to the rooms she had loved so well. In mid-May her family were summoned, and were with her for the last week.

On the morning of May 22nd she asked to see the local Protestant clergyman, but he was not available. To the little Roman Catholic nurse, who made an attempt at last-minute proselytising, she replied with her customary firmness: 'Never!' The family said the Lord's Prayer round her bed, and she appeared contented. She died in the night, having, her daughter-in-law assures me, the blessing of a quick and easy end.

XV

Aftermath

Her going made a stir, and on the whole a generous one. Mr de Valera was represented at her funeral, and the obituary notices did not merely see her as the Abbey co-founder and director, but acknowledged her importance as a creator in her own right.

The *Irish Times* quoted a critic who had pronounced: 'There is nothing in literature quite like her bewildered peasantry. Her stage creatures are so exquisitely helpless as to excite the sympathy of audiences everywhere.' It found a hidden seam of political and social satire in her work, and considered it 'somewhat remarkable that her three-act play for three characters, *Grania*, has never been staged'. Of the Abbey, it said that 'she was inspirer, founder, dramatist and director, from the conception of the enterprise until her death, and throughout all that long period she nursed the theatre as probably no one ever will again'. The leading article recognised the value to the literary movement of her passionate patriotism. 'If it had not captured her interest at the outset, the Irish literary revival — the germ of a movement which has become celebrated throughout the whole world — almost inevitably must have lost its Irish character within a very few years. She it was who ordained that the centre of the movement should become Dublin and not London.'

The London *Times*, while finding that 'her writing was best when the chosen form kept it within rather narrow limits', continued: 'it is not too much to say that her one-act plays — so humorous, so wise, so moving, so poetical even when most homely — are among the best in the language.'

The *Manchester Guardian* singled out her stage dialect for praise. 'There is a trot and rhythm in Kiltartanese; it is unique, unforgettable. The idiom owes its quaintness to the Gaelic, but there is nothing to beat the dignity, the humour, the eloquence, anon the absurdity of the common speech.' It held that 'Kiltartanese is purest and wildest in *Workhouse Ward*'. It also recognised that 'she collaborated with Yeats in writing the dialogue of *Kathleen ni Houlihan*, and the phrasing, as it stands, is hers.'

Yet within ten years, the writer of the remarkable letter to J. M. Hone was making the lament which I have already quoted. Here it is in full:

'She was the most complicated woman I can think of. Is no one going to write of her and keep her strange personality alive? Loving — cold. Womanly — cold. Enthusiastic — cold. Faithful — cold. Poetic — cold. Very calculating, dutiful, courageous, purposeful — all that built upon a bedrock sense of humour and love of fun and a bitter sarcasm, with a strong vein of simple coarseness of thought and simple inherited "protestantism". But there was a lot more in her than all that. All that seems to move only the surface, yet I perceive *no one* in Ireland cares in the very least about her. She is nearly forgotten already.'

'Cold' — the reiterated word indicates something ambiguous that puzzled Lady Shaw, but it would not have been so baffling to anyone who had a wider acquaintance with creative artists. There is in all of them a detachment which must inevitably strike the outsider as coldness, and which comes from their fundamental need to find out the truth, and then tell it, even if in the process other people may have to be hurt. 'Coldness' in this sense is present very strongly in both Yeats and Synge, but though they have it to a far greater degree than Lady Gregory (and are in consequence more complete artists), to contemporaries it is understandable that it appeared far more startling in an elderly woman than in younger men.

But in expressing astonishment at her being 'nearly forgotten' in, at any rate, literary Dublin — in County Galway she was never forgotten — Lady Shaw was perfectly justified, There was bound to be some reaction after her death against a writer who was so very much of an earlier generation, even though there was no topical element in her plays to make them seem dated. And the change of policy at the Abbey, which now had a free run with the removal of her hand and the weakening of Yeats's, also told against her work. But over and above all this, it seems to me that there was a conspiracy of denigration and banishment, directed against her principally because she was a woman, and that the door to it was opened by disloyalty on the part of the friend who could have done most to keep her memory alive and her plays on the stage.

2

Yeats, it is clear from his letters, meant to do something really handsome. He felt her death profoundly, writing on the morrow: 'I have lost one who has been to me for nearly forty years my strength and my conscience.' He missed Coole as 'the only place where I have ever had unbroken health'. Nor did the sorrow grow less; in 1936 he wrote to Lady Dorothy Wellesley: 'I long for quiet; long ago I used to find it at Coole. It was part of the genius of that house. Lady Gregory never rebelled like other Irish women I have known, who consumed themselves and their friends; in spite of Scripture she put the new wine into the old bottles.' He speaks several times of 'my *Life* of Lady Gregory', and collected letters and material for it.

The labour of such a work would have taken too much time from a poet whose creative genius was still powerful, and one can only be thankful that no full-dress biography came of the plan. What did come of it, however, was *Dramatis Personae*, an autobiographical sketch of his and her part in the founding of the literary movement, filled out to book-length by excerpts from his diaries and an account of his receiving the Nobel Prize. It was published in 1936, and according to his friend and biographer J. M. Hone constitutes his *monumentum perenne* for Lady Gregory. If so, it is a very curious monument indeed.

Some of its deficiencies I have already noted. It opens with an account of their meeting and a good deal of 'background material' on the Persse and Gregory families, by whose county status he seems considerably more impressed than ever she was herself. The Gregory record was an honourable one, but after all it had had nothing to do with her making, and the main claim to literary importance of both families was that the first produced a woman of outstanding gifts, and the second married her.

There follows an attractive, though typically self-centred, account of the *douceur de vivre* at Coole. ('My health was giving way, my nerves had been wrecked. Finding that I could not work, and thinking the open air salutary, Lady Gregory brought me from cottage to cottage collecting folklore,' etc.) Then comes the amusing story of the 'collaboration' with George Moore, and the work ends with the hailing of Lady Gregory as a 'creator' because she had discovered how to translate the sagas into Kiltartan.

That is all; no word of her turning playwright herself, or of her plays, though in *A People's Theatre*, his 'open letter' of 1919, he had spoken of 'that musical and delicate style that makes them always a fit accompaniment for verse' (he means, of course, makes them fit curtain-raisers for his verse plays), 'and sets them at times among the world's great comedies.' If *Dramatis Personae* is really her monument, this, surely, would have been the place to expand his appreciation of her plays? But the reader is left supposing that the only thing of significance she did was to supply him with the raw material of his own.

There are subtle, perhaps unconscious, detractions, both of her and of Synge. He tells us of Synge's egotism (a clear case of pot-and-kettle), and backs it up by the statement that Synge never paid a compliment to Lady Gregory or himself — demonstrably untrue in Lady Gregory's case. There is an anecdote to prove that Lady Gregory was not prudish, which leaves us with the impression that she *was* prudish, though in fact it is not about her at all but about two other people.

It seems to me that Lady Gregory is belittled by *Dramatis Personae*. The 'eternal monument' to her reputation turns out to be something much more like a tomb. It would be easier for the next commentator to take up where Yeats left off. Oliver Gogarty was not slow to follow the hint, and I have yet to hear of any protest being raised by Yeats.

It is not for me to analyse his motives, and indeed, the generous and the insincere were so intimately bound up in this extraordinary man that I doubt if anyone ever will. Yeats was complex, as genius of the first stature must be. All the human qualities were heightened in him, bad as well as good; to equate genius with nobility of conduct is a naïveté which should have been left behind in the Fourth Form. Its possessors are for the most part ruthless, and as the rest of us are on the whole expendable, I suppose this does not much signify in the ordinary way. It is only when genius comes up against lesser but very real talent that the unfairness of the elbowing-aside process strikes one. I have granted that while she lived, Lady Gregory derived more benefit than disadvantage from her contact with Yeats, though the extent of that benefit has been grossly exaggerated. I do not think it can be denied that her reputation was harmed by him after her death.

Far and away the best pages in *Dramatis Personae* are those in which Yeats pays off his old scores against Edward Martyn and George Moore. They are the second round in one of those glorious Irish slanging-matches which lull even the puritan English conscience out of its tiresome preoccupation with justice and truth. And how much more personally attractive is the Willie with his coat off than the stately W. B. Y. pontificating to the beglamoured disciples! We glimpse again the staunch and sardonic fighter who was Lady Gregory's comrade in arms, and of whom even those who did not like him very much now concede, as they look back over their memories, 'Yeats could sometimes be very good fun.'

3

With Lady Gregory dead and Yeats aging, the dangers inherent in the Abbey's acceptance of a state subsidy revealed themselves more clearly. Presently there was no personality on the directorate strong enough to stand up to Government pressure, and it is generally agreed that standards declined. Good actors were dismissed because they did not speak Irish, less competent ones engaged because they did, new plays were chosen for political rather than aesthetic merit. And many theatregoers, particularly those old enough to remember the standards set by the Fays and enforced by Yeats and Lady Gregory, maintain that this state of things persists today.

As an Englishwoman and a newcomer to the Abbey stalls, it is not for me to pass judgment; nor do I feel that the present company can fairly be judged as long as they are compelled to play in an unsuitable theatre, much larger than that for which the main body of the repertory was written. Fire gutted the interior of the Abbey in July of 1951, since when

they have been housed at the Queen's. There are elaborate
plans for rebuilding (although the shell of the time-honoured
building seems sound enough), but the auditorium of the
main theatre will not be much larger than the original, and
the acoustics, no doubt, greatly improved.

Having heard the company shout their way through a
tedious middle-class farce in a manner to make Sara Allgood
stop her ears and Frank Fay turn in his grave, I was prepared
to credit all I had heard of decline. But on my next visit, the
play was *The Scythe and the Sunset*, Mr Denis Johnston's
strong and thoughtful piece about the Easter Rising, and
these same actors brought to it a virile attack and a period
sense which seemed to me magnificent. The only weakness
was the patently Irish actor in the minor part of an English
officer; the Abbey should keep a true-born Englishman on
its roster to play the villains. It seems probable that the
company is as good as the work it is given to do, and that this
pre-eminently dramatists' theatre is a dramatists' theatre still.

My chief quarrel with the present directorate is that Lady
Gregory's plays have been largely allowed to drop out of the
repertory in English, except for the inevitable *Rising of the
Moon*. The rest of the *Seven Short Plays* get rare revivals,
Dervorgilla has been given three times since her death, *Damer's
Gold* and *The Canavans* once. In Irish translation, however,
the one-acters are still used as part of the theatre's policy of
fostering the language. I can believe that 'Kiltartan', being
based on Gaelic syntax, translates easily, but the claim that
Lady Gregory's plays are 'better' in a language other than that
in which she wrote them is disingenuous. In any case, they
are thereby rendered incomprehensible to foreign visitors, and
also (judging by the proportion of the audience that leaves
before the Irish tailpiece) to a good number of those who
have enjoyed the benefit of compulsory Irish at school.

But admittedly the Queen's is not the right theatre for

Lady Gregory's rather delicate line. Hers are the last plays that should be shouted; they require of producer and cast an intimate, affectionate approach, a phrasing as careful as that of a Mozart symphony. I feel sure there is already the talent there to interpret them; perhaps, by the time the Abbey is home again, there will also be the good will.

4

As to the matter of the Lane Pictures, for twenty-seven years after Lady Gregory's death the butter remained in the dog's mouth, increasing relentlessly in value year by year; Hugh Lane, who could always make money by his flair, continued to make it from the grave. And most of us in England who knew the facts of the case continued to be unhappy in our possession of treasures which were legally ours but morally another country's. We valued the English reputation for honesty, and felt ourselves shamed by what Dr Vere Gregory has finely called 'England's Thirty-Nine Articles of Bad Faith'.

Naturally, Ireland did not let the matter rest. The Epstein bust of Lady Gregory in the Dublin Municipal Gallery seemed to urge the visitor towards the inmost room, whose walls were eloquently bare except for one canvas, the big Orpen portrait of Sir Hugh Lane. There is much of interest in the gallery, particularly in the way of contemporary Irish painting and sculpture, but lacking the Lane bequest it was poor in modern French pictures, and reproached the riches at the Tate.

A positive though shockingly unofficial attempt to secure justice was made on April 12th, 1956, when Paul Hogan, a twenty-five-year-old Irish student, walked out of the Tate with the Berthe Morisot 'Jour d'Eté' tucked under his arm while an accomplice, Bill Fogarty, kept watch, and the passers-by took no notice. (A *Punch* cartoon a few days later showed an Irishman leaving the Tate with its indignant Director tucked under his arm, and the passers-by still taking no notice.) The Irish National Students' Council immediately claimed full responsibility for the action, and stated that twenty-two members had shared in its planning.

For four days the picture was missing and the Lane affair made the headlines, receiving more publicity than ever Lady Gregory had been able to get for it. Questions were asked in the House, and some of them made reference to her part in the struggle. Meanwhile rumour traced the Morisot to Dublin and to Paris. On the 16th a woman handed it over to the Irish Embassy in London, whence the Tate retrieved it unharmed.

The theft was of course a gesture, and while there still seemed a possibility that the picture might have been smuggled across to Dublin, a Corporation official had stated very properly that 'we could not accept a picture stolen in such a manner'. For all that, I suspect that many on both sides of the channel were disappointed that Dublin did not have the chance, and that Lady Gregory would have been among them. When a project of lending the pictures to Dublin had been mooted, she had written to Yeats that 'if we get the pictures to this side, of course we will never let them go back'. Messrs Fogarty and Hogan would surely have been heroes right after her heart.

At length, on November 12th, 1959, a compromise solution was announced simultaneously in the House of Commons and the Dail. The Lane Pictures were to be divided into two groups of roughly equal value, and first one half, then the other, were to be lent for exhibition in Dublin during four successive periods of five years each. The arrangement is to be reviewed at the end of the twenty years, and there seems every likelihood that it will become a permanent one. The Irish Prime Minister and the leaders of the Opposition parties welcomed it as an honourable compromise in a prolonged and difficult controversy, and held that it would 'to a considerable extent secure that the wishes of the late Sir Hugh Lane were carried out'.

That Lady Gregory would have been fully satisfied is doubtful. We have seen her views on the matter of a loan, and when at one point it was suggested to her that the National Gallery might be more likely to give up the pictures if offered a 'present' of one or two, she had replied stoutly that there could never be any question of partition, and that not an inch of canvas should be sacrificed. Nevertheless, there are other instances in which her woman's sense of the feasible made her thankful for what she could get, while in no way renouncing her ultimate determination to have full justice; and to see the walls of the Lane room clothed at last, even if with technically borrowed splendour, must be in some measure comforting to her ghost.

5

The economic difficulties of the Irish Republic have this for compensation, that the Irish countryside has been largely spared the hideous suburban building that is devouring the English. Lady Gregory's County Galway is much as she left it, and only at Coole itself would she find drastic change.

The grey elegance of Galway City is scarcely spoiled by the modern shopfronts along its narrow main street. The side streets are mysterious and beautiful with merchant princes' mansions and warehouses, many, alas, derelict. The Spanish Gate still presides over quays as wide as those of some Hanseatic town, though a larger and steadier steamer than Synge's now leaves thrice a week for the Aran Islands.

The vernacular drama which began with the Coole Punch-and-Judy show and Hyde's plays for the Galway *feis* is now maintained by the only full-time vernacular theatre in the whole Celtic world. The history of this gallant venture runs in many ways parallel to that of its great sister the Abbey, and its present leader, Professor Murphy of University College, Galway combines in his person the toughness, guile, and galvanic organising powers of a Lady Gregory and a Yeats. A modest Government grant makes it possible to pay the producer and the stage carpenter; the rest give their services free, or for a tiny payment to cover the expenses of attending rehearsals. They are thus amateurs by status, but professional in their standards of performance and production. The theatre relies for its repertory mainly on translations of English, French and Spanish plays, but like the Abbey puts the discovery of original playwriting talent among its first objects. It is not, and has resisted all attempts to make it, a mere Irish conversation-class.

The Galway building most closely associated with Lady Gregory's plays has vanished, and apart from this association, it is not a loss to be lamented. The gaol has been pulled down, and its site is being used for the building of a new Roman Catholic cathedral. The only monument in the city to its most distinguished daughter is the simple slab in the new Cemetery; the lapidary inscription, 'She Shall be Remembered For Ever,' is more likely than most to be true. Eyre Square, which like many Irish squares is so large as to be almost a park, contains a whimsical and much-photographed statue to Padraig O Conaire, the vernacular poet. There would be ample room on the opposite side for some memorial to Lady Gregory, or an even more appropriate site would be down by the Spanish Gate, on the quays which her Sergeant and her Ragged Man will haunt eternally. I call the attention of the citizens to an omission they should surely repair.

Gort and Loughrea are even less altered, and their atmosphere, so reminiscent of similar small French towns, will

enchant the visitor in search of the real rural Ireland, free
from tourist self-consciousness. Loughrea, even less of a
tourist centre than Gort, should by reason of its cathedral be
visited by all who would appreciate the full creative richness
of the Irish Renascence, and Edward Martyn's exquisite little
parish church at Ardrahan is but a few miles' run through the
country lanes.

A considerable part of the Roxborough ruin stands,
including one high gable and a chimney that must presently
crash in some Atlantic gale. But today one would be hard put
to it to fix the date of the conflagration; it might have been
in the seventeenth century. What fire did not devour, the
'Gothick' gatehouse and turrets, is buried under mountains of
ivy. In the huge empty kitchen-garden one can trace the beds
where the little Augusta filched her strawberries, and a few
fruit-trees dangle matted and sterile from the walls.

The estate of the Persses has been parcelled out among a
hundred and twenty smallholdings, each with its neat grey
box of a house, but they are lost in that landscape of hillocks.
Most seem prosperous, though a few stand empty. The
occupant of the farm directly under the Roxborough ruin is
something of a philosopher; he ended a recital of his agricultural tribulations with the comment: 'Ah, sure, what good
would it do you to be the richest man in the graveyard?' The
pithy turn of phrase which was Lady Gregory's inspiration
still comes readily to her neighbours.

The Protestant church on the estate has utterly vanished,
even to the foundations. Nothing remains but the graveyard,
with decent simple memorials half obliterated by brambles.
They were tended till recently, I was told, but there is no
Protestant family left to care for them now. A little apart
from the others, its capital letters eaten away by frost and
rain, lies the grave of Lady Gregory's mother, Frances
Persse.

6

The House of Coole stood empty for a good many years, and then was sold by the Forestry Department to a contractor, who demolished it for the value of the building stone. The knocker of the front door was presented as a keepsake to the Abbey green-room, and the handsome brass door-knob to Bernard Shaw. It may be seen by National Trust visitors to Shaw's Corner at Ayot St. Lawrence.

Most who have written of Yeats and Lady Gregory express indignation that the house was not kept as a literary shrine. This feeling I cannot share. Literary shrines seem to me on the whole to fail of their effect; I find myself closer to Wordsworth and Dorothy by reading her Journals than by visiting Dove Cottage. Beautiful and historic though Coole Park may have been, it was the woman who made the soul of the house, not the house the soul of the woman. It was primarily for her, and not for the lake and the woods and the creature comforts, that Yeats and the rest of them came. It would have been unreasonable to expect the Gregory family to leave the books and furnishings behind, and it would have been a costly house for the Irish Government to maintain. Besides, I cannot help remembering the rats.

In any case, woods and lake form an adequate object of pilgrimage. They are little changed, except that under the Forestry Department there is denser planting of conifers, and that cows and sheep graze all through the estate, bringing with them flies. The main gate into the tunnel-like ilex avenue is locked, but there is a stile beside it, and the visitor may walk the remaining half-mile along the winding drive through the woods. Presently he emerges into an open space beside the horseshoe-shaped paddock; here the house stood, but all that remains is a hole in the ground, floored with concrete, which was the floor of the porch. Red-brick ruins some way to the right were dairies. Further to the right again, a double-gate leads into what was the pleasure-garden. The path alongside the great border, where Yeats walked and composed, is still edged with box, now grown knee-high, and though the plants have gone, the flowering shrubs survive. One who visits Coole at all times of the year tells me that he never fails to find a bouquet in Lady Gregory's garden.

The Autograph Tree rises half-way down this path, on the edge of what is still recognisably a lawn. Unsolicited contributions continuing to add themselves, it was ultimately surrounded by a high wire cage. This makes it difficult to read the significant autographs, while in no way discouraging the more athletic from their self-commemoration.

A track along the left-hand edge of the paddock, flanked now by a dense pinewood, takes one in ten minutes more to the lake, and after the mile of forest its wide silvery expanse comes as even more of a relief than it must have been in Yeats's day. His muster of nine-and-fifty swans can be easily made up; it is the poet, not they, who has 'flown away'. They have in fact been multiplying, and the foresters now estimate that there are at least a hundred breeding pairs.

And it is, I am aware, the poet who is chiefly remembered by those who wander over the rather dank brown-velvet moss of the lake shores. It is a setting better suited to his cold genius than to her warm talent. The echoes she has left behind her are the voices of living men and women, and to me at least, they speak more strongly in the placid square of Gort, the bustling streets of Galway, the companionable mingling of old and new dust at the Seven Churches, the gaunt hamlets on the slopes of Slieve Echtge, than ever they do in Coole.

Gort's wide main street is still, except for a new shopfront or two, so exactly the Cloon of Lady Gregory's plays that at any moment Mr Nestor may come sauntering along with *Tit-Bits* under his arm, or Mrs Delane scurry out with the latest news culled from the postcards. The old men sunning themselves on seats along the pavement look benign enough, but let family pride be affronted and they would at once, one feels, break into the brilliant vituperation of their ancestors in the Workhouse Ward. On the Galway quays the ballad-singer fights for the soul of the sergeant, and at one of those quayside inns, Sarsfield fights for the soul of King James. MacDonough's pipes stop the traffic of the traders, as Raftery's did before them, and as you descend from the ring of Connemara you meet wild-looking girls like his Catherine, with the wind blowing from them the shawl. In some tumbledown cabin the chimney-sweeps are trembling at myths of their own making, and in some comfortable farmhouse Dave is healed by a woman's faith.

Slieve Echtge is remote as ever, one of the loneliest hill-tracts in Ireland, where the howling of the Atlantic wind might still bring you the mountain mother's triumph in her son's heroic death. Or maybe Grania's one truth too many, echoing forlornly across the centuries:

He had no love for me at any time. It is easy know it now. His desire was all the time with you yourself, and Almhuin.

Lady Gregory's Principal Publications

1894   *Autobiography of Sir William Gregory*, edited by Lady Gregory. (Murray.)

1898   *Mr Gregory's Letter Box*, edited by Lady Gregory. (Murray.)

1902   *Cuchulain of Muirthemne*. (Murray.)

1903   *Poets and Dreamers*. (Murray.)

1904   *Gods and Fighting Men*. (Murray.)

1905   *Kincora*, first version. (Abbey Theatre Publications.)

1907   *A Book of Saints and Wonders*. (Murray.)

1909   *Seven Short Plays: Spreading the News, Hyacinth Halvey, The Rising of the Moon, The Jackdaw, The Workhouse Ward, The Travelling Man, The Gaol Gate*. (Maunsel.)
The Kiltartan History Book. (Maunsel.)

1910   *The Image*. (Maunsel.)
The Kiltartan Wonder Book, illustrated by Margaret Gregory. (Maunsel.)
The Kiltartan Molière. (Maunsel.)

1912   *Irish Folk-History Plays*, first series: *Kincora, Grania, Dervorgilla*. (Putnam.)
Irish Folk-History Plays, second series: *The Canavans, The White Cockade, The Deliverer*. (Putnam.)

1913   *New Comedies: The Bogie Men, The Full Moon, Coats, Damer's Gold, MacDonough's Wife*. (Putnam.)

1914   *Our Irish Theatre*. (Putnam.)

1916   *The Golden Apple*, illustrated by Margaret Gregory. (Murray.)

1918   *The Kiltartan Poetry Book*. (Putnam.)

1920   *Visions and Beliefs in the West of Ireland*. (Putnam.)

1921   *Hugh Lane's Life and Achievement, with some account of the Dublin Galleries*. (Murray.)

1922   *The Image* and other plays: *The Image, Hanrahan's Oath, Shanwalla, The Wrens*. (Putnam.)

1923   *Three Wonder Plays: The Dragon, Aristotle's Bellows, The Jester*. (Putnam.)

1924   *The Story Brought by Brigit*. (Putnam.)

1926   *On the Racecourse.* (Talbot Press.)
       A Case for the Return of Hugh Lane's Pictures to Dublin.
       (Talbot Press.)
1928   *Three Last Plays: Sancho's Master, Dave, The Doctor in*
       Spite of Himself. (Putnam.)
1930   *My First Play: Colman and Guaire.* (Mathews and Marrot.)
1931   *Coole.* (Cuala Press.)
1946   *Lady Gregory's Journals.* A selection edited by Lennox
       Robinson. (Putnam.)

Bibliography

Blunt, Wilfrid Scawen. *Diaries*, 1921 edition, with preface by Lady Gregory.

O'Casey, Sean. *Inishfallen, Fare Thee Well.* 1949.

Ellis-Fermor, Una. *The Irish Dramatic Movement.* 1939.

Fahy, Dr Jerome. *History and Antiquities of the Diocese of Kilmacduagh.* 1893.

Fay, Gerard. *The Abbey Theatre, Cradle of Genius.* 1957.

Fay, W. G. *The Fays of the Abbey Theatre.* 1935.

Gonne, Maud. *A Servant of the Queen.* 1938.

O'Grady, Standish H. *Silva Gadelica.* 1892.

Greene, Professor David H. *J. M. Synge.* 1959.

Gregory, Dr Vere H. *The House of Gregory.* 1943.

Gwynn, Denis. *Edward Martyn and the Irish Revival.* 1930.

Hone, J. M. *W. B. Yeats.* 1942.

Hyde, Douglas. *Beside the Fire.* 1890.
    Love Songs of Connacht. 1893.

MacLiammoir, Micheal. *All for Hecuba.* 1946.

Moore, George. *Ave.* 1911.
    Vale. 1914.

Pogson, Rex. *Miss Horniman and the Gaiety Theatre.* 1952.

Robinson, Lennox. *Ireland's Abbey Theatre.* 1951.

Shiubhlaigh, Maire nic. *The Splendid Years.* 1955.

Synge, J. M. *The Aran Islands.* 1906.

Yeats, W. B. *The Celtic Twilight.* 1893.
    The Cutting of an Agate. 1919.
    Plays, ed. 1922.
    Dramatis Personae. 1936.
    Letters, ed. Allan Wade. 1954.

INDEX

Index

PRINTED IN GREAT BRITAIN
BY ROBERT MACLEHOSE AND CO. LTD
THE UNIVERSITY PRESS, GLASGOW